Heroic Chancellor:
Winston Churchill and the University of Bristol 1929–65

To the Chancellors and Vice-Chancellors of the University of Bristol
past, present and future

Heroic Chancellor:
Winston Churchill and the University of Bristol 1929–65

David Cannadine

LONDON
INSTITUTE OF HISTORICAL RESEARCH

Published by
UNIVERSITY OF LONDON
SCHOOL OF ADVANCED STUDY
INSTITUTE OF HISTORICAL RESEARCH
Senate House, Malet Street, London WC1E 7HU

© David Cannadine 2016
All rights reserved

This text was first published by the University of Bristol in 2015.

ISBN 978 1 909646 18 6

**I never had the advantage of
a university education.**

Winston Churchill, speech on accepting an honorary degree
at the University of Copenhagen, 10 October 1950

**The privilege of a university education
is a great one; the more widely it is
extended the better for any country.**

Winston Churchill, Foundation Day Speech,
University of London, 18 November 1948

**I always enjoy coming to Bristol and
performing my part in this ceremony,
so dignified and so solemn, and yet so
inspiring and reverent.**

Winston Churchill, Chancellor's address,
University of Bristol, 26 November 1954

Contents

Preface	ix
List of abbreviations	xi
List of illustrations	xiii
Introduction	1
1. 'Uneducated' Chancellor	5
2. Appointed Chancellor	13
3. Apprentice Chancellor	23
4. Wartime Chancellor	33
5. Opposition Chancellor	45
6. Premier Chancellor	55
7. Sunset Chancellor	65
Conclusion	73
Index	77

Preface

To commemorate the fiftieth anniversary, in January 2015, of the death of the most extraordinary and heroic figure ever to be closely and directly associated with it, the University of Bristol arranged and hosted a series of public lectures in the spring of that year, covering many facets of Sir Winston Churchill's remarkably varied life; and I was kindly invited to speak on one aspect of it, which had a particular local appeal and domestic resonance, namely his long years and his diverse activities as Chancellor of the University, extending from 1929 until 1965. This was an irresistible invitation, since not only was Churchill the most illustrious and the most distinguished Chancellor that the University of Bristol has ever had, but he was also in his prime, from 1940 onwards, probably the most famous and the most distinguished chancellor of any university anywhere in the world.

I am deeply grateful to the vice-chancellor of the University of Bristol, Professor Sir Eric Thomas, for asking me to deliver that lecture, initially in Bristol and subsequently in London, which was a much-abridged version of the text that follows here. In preparing both the original talk and this more extended essay, I am also most indebted to Sophie Hatchwell and Martha Vandrei for their essential research assistance, to the archivists of the Universities of Aberdeen and Bristol and of Churchill College, Cambridge for their help, to Dr Martin Crossley-Evans for reading an earlier draft, and to Emily Morrell and Jane Winters for seeing the manuscript through to publication. I additionally express my thanks to Allen Packwood, the Director of the Churchill Archives Centre at Churchill College, Cambridge, for his help and support; and also, and for many reasons, to Linda Colley, not least because she is both a graduate and an honorary graduate of what it seems appropriate in this context to describe as Churchill's University.

DNC
Princeton University
April 2016

List of abbreviations

Names
UoB   University of Bristol
WSC   Winston Spencer Churchill, Chancellor of the University of Bristol 1929–65
TTL   Dr. Thomas Tudor Loveday, Vice-Chancellor of the University of Bristol 1922–44, and acting part-time Vice-Chancellor 1944–45
PRM   Professor Sir Philip Morris, Vice-Chancellor of the University of Bristol 1946–66

Printed sources
Bristol   D. Carleton, *A University for Bristol: A History in Text and Pictures* (Bristol, 1986 edn.)
C&G, i–viii   R. S. Churchill & M. Gilbert, *Winston S Churchill* (8 vols., London, 1966–88)
MEL   W. S. Churchill, *My Early Life: A Roving Commission* ([1930] London, 1989 edn.)
Speeches, vi–viii R. Rhodes James (ed.), *Winston S. Churchill: His Complete Speeches* (vols. vi-viii, New York, 1974)

Archival sources
CHAR   Churchill papers pre-1945, Churchill Archives Centre, Churchill College, Cambridge
CHUR   Churchill papers post-1945, Churchill Archives Centre, Churchill College, Cambridge
UoBSC   Special Collections, Arts and Social Sciences Library, University of Bristol

List of illustrations

1. The Churchill coat of arms on display in the Queen's Building, University of Bristol. — xiv
2. Churchill wearing his robes as Chancellor of the Exchequer, drawn by John Singer Sargent, *c*.1925. — 6
3. Dr. Thomas Loveday, Vice Chancellor, 1922–44. — 14
4. Churchill borne shoulder-high by undergraduates on his first visit to Bristol as Chancellor, December 1929. — 19
5. The Great Hall of the Wills Memorial Building before bomb damage. — 34
6. The Great Hall after bomb damage in December 1940. — 35
7. The Chancellor with Robert Menzies and Gil Winant, having conferred honorary degrees on them, April 1941. — 37
8. Churchill receiving the Freedom of Bristol at the Council Chambers, April 1945 — 41
9. The Chancellor with Ernest Bevin and A. V. Alexander, having conferred honorary degrees on them, April 1945. — 42
10. Sir Philip Morris, Vice-Chancellor, 1946–66. — 46
11. The Chancellor with leading figures from the universities of the British Empire and Commonwealth, having conferred honorary degrees on them, July 1948. — 51
12. Churchill after addressing students in Colston Hall, November 1954. — 56
13. The Chancellor laying the foundation stone of the Queen's Building, December 1951. — 58
14. Churchill conferring an honorary degree on R. A. Butler during his last visit as Chancellor, November 1954. — 62
15. Churchill unveiling a plaque in the Queen's Building, November 1954. — 64
16. Churchill in his Chancellor's robes, painted by Sir Frank Salisbury, *c*.1943. — 66
17. Order of Service, Bristol Cathedral, January 1965. — 71

SIR WINSTON CHURCHILL
CHANCELLOR OF THE UNIVERSITY
1929–1965

Figure 1. The Churchill coat of arms on display in the Queen's Building, University of Bristol.

Introduction

In early March 1965, only a few weeks after the death of Sir Winston Churchill, which had taken place in mid January that year, a somewhat disgruntled and disappointed graduate of the University of Bristol wrote to remonstrate with Sir Philip Morris, the Vice-Chancellor, who would soon be retiring after twenty distinguished years in post. The disaffected alumnus had been concerned to 'leave a decent interval since the passing of our late Chancellor', but at the risk of 'complaining prematurely', he now felt compelled to write. It had, he started in, 'been a most unhappy reflection that', as far as he had been able to discover, 'in the whole of the obituary notices to the late Sir Winston Churchill, there has not been a single reference to the fact that he was Chancellor of Bristol University'. To make matters worse, he continued, 'a very new institution like the new science college at Cambridge of only a few years standing', by which he meant Churchill College, established by Royal Charter in 1960 as the national memorial, 'should have taken not only a share of the glory of association with Sir Winston Churchill, but almost the whole of it from Bristol'. Surely, he went on, 'it is not naive to have expected that a term of office of some thirty-six years would have received some recognition'. Of course, he added, 'I realize that nothing can now be done to set matters right, and it is doubtful if such remedy either is or ever was in the hands of anyone except Sir Winston Churchill himself'. He was writing, he insisted, 'not in a spirit of criticism,' but because he could 'not help feeling a little hurt by the way these events have gone'. And he ended by expressing his interest in knowing 'if my interpretation of these events is correct'. On the other hand, he concluded, he would 'be more than pleased' if his 'interpretation was wrong'.[1]

Replying on behalf of the Vice-Chancellor, the Registrar produced a tactful but firm reply. 'I think', he began, 'I can remember you at the University in 1952, but after this interval I am not sure whether I have got the right man'. If so, he went on, 'it is very pleasant to renew acquaintance, but in any case it is agreeable to hear of your interest'. The position of Churchill College, Cambridge was, he acknowledged, 'indeed special', and there was no getting away from that. Perhaps, too, living as he did in Rochdale, the author of the letter had 'for some time

---

[1] UoBSC DM 1571/38: B. E. Holden to PRM, 7 March 1965. For a further letter of complaint see UoBSC DM 1571/38: S. T. Willcox to Mrs H. M. Willoughby, 28 July 1965.

been out of touch with what goes on in the University'? In fact, the Registrar continued, Sir Winston's Chancellorship 'was very much in the minds of people in this part of the country'. Churchill had supported Bristol's latest appeal, launched in 1962, and the Registrar enclosed the booklet published in connection with it, 'in case your copy did not reach you'. On the great man's death, the City and the University had 'jointly arranged a very impressive memorial service in the Cathedral', and plans were already afoot to establish a special fund which would pay for the annual celebration of the late Chancellor's birthday at the University hall of residence that was named after him, which would serve as 'a permanent memorial of an appropriate kind'. (A further memorial would be unveiled to him in the Queen's Building in April 1966.[2]) The Registrar was not sure 'whether you will feel that this is an entirely satisfactory answer to your letter', but he hoped that at least it would show his interest in the points his correspondent had raised. 'It is', he concluded, 'always pleasant to keep in touch with people who have been at the University, though I know the difficulties caused by shortage of time and length of journey to Bristol'.[3]

Half a century on, it is impossible to know whether the complainant was mollified by this well-mannered but unyielding response. Either way, and as this exchange makes plain, Churchill does not loom large in the important and significant history of the University of Bristol, any more than the University of Bristol looms large in the many-sided and brightly-lit tableau of Churchill's extraordinary life.[4] As figureheads and ceremonial cynosures, the roles of university chancellors are very properly more ornamental than fundamental. Moreover Churchill had not been educated at university, and his appointment to the Bristol Chancellorship in 1929 came as a surprise to many people, himself included. During the 1930s, according to Sir Philip Morris, 'he did not so easily or so naturally assume either the Chancellor's role or the Chancellor's robes', and if he had died in 1939, he would, in the words of Bristol's historian, 'have gone down in the nation's history as a failed politician, and in the University's history as a Chancellor whose term of office had no particular significance'.[5] That is, perhaps, a slightly harsh and exaggerated view; but there can be no doubt that, as a public figure no less than as Bristol's Chancellor, Churchill's position was dramatically and triumphantly transformed in 1940; and thereafter the University could

---

[2] UoBSC DM 1571/38: H. C. Butterfield to Professor Harris, 27 April 1966.
[3] UoBSC DM 1571/38: Registrar to B. E. Holden, 10 March 1965.
[4] In *C&G*, v–viii, there are only 13 entries, including those to both the University and the City of Bristol.
[5] UoBSC DM 1571/38: PRM, recollections of WSC, 22 July 1953, p. 1; *Bristol*, p. 98.

proudly (and unexpectedly?) boast as its senior officer the man widely regarded as 'the savour of his country' and 'the greatest Englishman of his time'.[6] For the next fifteen years, Bristol would bask in the reflected glory of his lustre and renown, and in the Corinthian splendour and gusto of his personality; but during the last, sad decade of his life, Churchill effectively withdrew from active involvement in the University's affairs. Even before his death, this meant his Chancellorship was already becoming an increasingly distant memory, albeit a memory warmly cherished by those who could, indeed, remember it.

Yet while Churchill's association with the University of Bristol is both history and biography in a relatively minor key, it is also (to shift the metaphor) much more than a mere twentieth-century footnote to the development of an important institution of higher learning and the unfolding drama of a remarkable life. This is partly because the relevant archival material, both at the University of Bristol and in the archives of Churchill College, Cambridge, is of considerable abundance and serious interest. It is also undeniable that Churchill was Bristol's greatest Chancellor, serving for longer than anyone who came before or after him, playing the part with unrivalled brio and élan, and giving the University an enhanced public profile which none of his forebears or successors has ever rivalled. But it took Churchill some time to learn what he could and could not do as Chancellor, and how he should set about doing it. Even so, the University did help sustain him during the 1930s when many people wrote him off as finished, and he ever after remained grateful for that.[7] And the experience he gained from his early involvement with Bristol would be especially valuable when, in his later years of power, fame and glory, he delivered major speeches at universities across the United Kingdom, western Europe and the United States. Towards the end of his life, he was, indeed, more intimately involved with the foundation of Churchill College, Cambridge, and he also supported the establishment of the University of Essex, the county that encompassed his Woodford parliamentary constituency.[8] But Churchill's association with the University of Bristol was longer and closer than with any other place of higher learning; he invested his activities there, like everything he touched, with energy and excitement, glamour and showmanship, a sense of occasion and a love of the limelight, and in the

---

[6] I. Berlin, *Mr. Churchill in 1940* (n.d.), p. 39; A. J. P. Taylor, *English History, 1914–1945* (Oxford, 1965), p. 29, note 1.

[7] UoBSC DM 1571/38: PRM, recollections of WSC, 22 July 1953, p. 2.

[8] J. J. Walsh, 'Postgraduate technological education in Britain: events leading up to the establishment of Churchill College, Cambridge, 1950–1958', *Minerva*, xxxvi (1998), 147–77; CHUR 2/55: Sir John Ruggles Brise to WSC, 1 April 1964.

pages that follow, that remarkable and unique relationship is, for the first time, set out in full.⁹

---

⁹ R. Hyam, *Elgin and Churchill at the Colonial Office, 1905–1908: the Watershed of the Empire-Commonwealth* (1968), pp. 497–501.

1. 'Uneducated' Chancellor

At almost exactly the same time that he would be appointed Chancellor of the University of Bristol, Winston Churchill was turning his attention to writing *My Early Life*, his classic autobiography of youthful misfortune and adolescent adventure, which by turns would be a nostalgic account of late nineteenth-century aristocratic privilege and imperial confidence, of life as a cavalry officer in the heyday of the Raj, and of soldiering on the frontiers of Empire and beyond. But by no stretch of the imagination was it the work of a man who was obviously qualified to be the Chancellor of any British university, let alone Bristol in particular. For on the contrary, and with some good cause, Churchill depicted and described himself in those pages as 'an uneducated man'.[1] Indeed, and as he went on to demonstrate, in a formal sense he had scarcely been educated at all, having been unhappy and unsuccessful at his preparatory and public schools, and never having been deemed clever or motivated enough to attempt applying to, or attend, university. Throughout the opening chapters of *My Early Life*, Churchill described himself as a 'troublesome boy', who resented headmasterly authority, disliked rote learning, hated examinations, felt 'menaced with education', and regarded his schooldays as 'the only barren and unhappy period of my life, an unending spell, of worries that did not then seem petty, and of toil un-cheered by fruition; a time of discomfort, restriction and purposeless monotony'.[2] He was miserable at a succession of preparatory schools, and wretched when he moved on to Harrow, where he only stayed for four-and-a-half years. He was hopeless at mathematics, no better at Latin, and never got anywhere with Greek, as evidenced by his observation that 'Mr. Gladstone read Homer for fun, which I thought served him right'.[3] (By contrast, his father, Lord Randolph Churchill, had been to Eton, and for much longer than Winston was at Harrow, and he went on to Merton College, Oxford, where he read history and graduated with high second-class honours, and according to his college tutor, he might have become a professional historian.)[4]

It has long been recognised that Winston Churchill retrospectively exaggerated his scholarly and academic shortcomings in *My Early Life*: he

---

[1] *C&G*, v, pp. 362–5; *MEL*, p. 130.
[2] *MEL*, p. 52.
[3] *MEL*, pp. 17, 37.
[4] R. F. Foster, *Lord Randolph Churchill: a Political Life* (Oxford, 1981), p. 12.

Figure 2. Churchill wearing his robes as Chancellor of the Exchequer, drawn by John Singer Sargent, c.1925.

may have been a born rebel, and he was undoubtedly poor at mathematics and the classics, but he showed great promise in English and history, and his memory was already exceptionally good.⁵ Nevertheless, his generally low level of interest and attainment throughout his unhappy schooldays was the despair of many of his masters. One of them reported to Lady Randolph Churchill that Winston was 'constantly late for school, losing his books and papers – he is so regular in his irregularity that I really don't know what to do; and sometimes think he cannot help it'.⁶ And when he finally scraped into the Royal Military College at Sandhurst, where the academic requirements were decidedly undemanding, but only doing so at the third attempt, Lord Randolph wrote his wayward and disappointing son a cruel and devastating letter, denouncing the

> slovenly, happy-go-lucky, harum-scarum style of work for which you have always been distinguished at your different schools. Never have I received a really good report of your conduct in your work from any master or tutor you had from time to time to do with ... If you cannot prevent yourself from leading the idle, useless, unprofitable life you have had during your schooldays, you will become a mere social wastrel, and you will degenerate into a shabby, unhappy and futile existence. If that is so, you will have to bear all the blame for such misfortunes yourself.⁷

When he penned these chilling words, Lord Randolph had less than eighteen months to live, but the impact of this letter on his son was deep and lifelong. Much of the energy and ambition and determination that Winston would later display came from a determination to prove Lord Randolph wrong (in his greatest moment of triumph, on V.E. Day in 1945, he wished that his father had been present to see he had made something of his life); and in the short run, this letter may have spurred him on to try to make some effort to remedy his educational deficiencies.⁸

This Churchill duly did when he was serving as a cavalry officer with his regiment in Bangalore in India.⁹ It was, he later recalled, in the 'winter of 1896, when I had almost completed my twenty-second year, that the desire for learning came upon me', and that he discovered 'mental needs that now began to press insistently':

> I knew of course that youths at universities were stuffed with all this patter at nineteen and twenty ... We never set much store by them or their affected

⁵ *MEL*, p. 27; *C&G*, i. pp. 184–5.
⁶ *C&G*, i. pp. 114–15.
⁷ *C&G*, i,. pp. 196–8.
⁸ *C&G*, viii. p. 372.
⁹ *C&G*, i. 333–9.

superiority, remembering that they were only at their books, while we were commanding men and guarding the Empire. Nevertheless, I had sometimes resented the apt and copious information which some of them seemed to possess, and I now wished I could find a competent teacher whom I could listen to and cross-examine for an hour or so every day.[10]

But there were no teachers to be found or to be had in Bangalore, and so young Winston decided to educate himself during those long, hot, lazy afternoons when his fellow cavalry officers were merely resting:

I resolved to read history, philosophy, economics, and things like that; and I wrote to my mother, asking for such books as I had heard of on these topics. She responded with alacrity, and every month the mail brought me a substantial package of what I thought were standard works.[11]

For two years, he subjected himself to a punishing, but not always discerning, schedule of self-education and self-improvement: 'from November to May,' he noted, 'I read four or five hours every day: Plato's *Republic*, the *Politics of* Aristotle, Schopenhauer on Pessimism, Malthus on Population, and Darwin's *Origin of Species*: all interspersed with other books of lesser standing.[12]

This was, as Churchill later admitted, 'a curious education'. He approached it with 'an empty, hungry mind, and with fairly strong jaws; and what I got I bit'. But there was no one to offer him guidance as to which books and authors were important, and which were not, and he began, 'for the first time to envy those young cubs at the university, who had fine scholars to tell them what was what'.[13] Indeed, for a brief period he contemplated applying to Oxford in a further attempt to remedy the educational deficiencies of which he was becoming ever more aware. But he would have been obliged to pass examinations in the classical languages, and after the experience of commanding British troops on the borders of Empire, he could not face the prospect of 'toiling at Greek irregular verbs'; and so, 'after much pondering', he 'had to my keen regret to put the plan aside'. Nevertheless, Churchill's regret at not having been to university was lifelong, as were the insecurities that came with it.[14] When he finally entered the House of Commons, to pursue the career in public life on which he had set his heart, he found himself up against many men who were far better

---

[10] *MEL*, p. 123.
[11] *MEL*, p. 124.
[12] *MEL*, p. 126.
[13] *MEL*, pp. 126–7.
[14] P. Addison, *Churchill: The Unexpected Hero* (Oxford, 2005), p. 14; *MEL*, p. 217.

educated than he had been, among them Asquith and Balfour in an older generation, and F.E. Smith and Leopold Amery among his contemporaries. This put him at a distinct disadvantage, and one of the reasons his speeches were so elaborate and carefully prepared was that he 'never had the practice which comes to young men at the University of speaking impromptu on all sorts of subjects'.[15] And one of the reasons he filled so many of his books with extended quotations from primary sources was that he wanted to be taken seriously as a writer and an historian by people with university degrees and academic qualifications. But the Oxbridge-educated statesmen did criticise and they did condescend. 'Winston', Arthur Balfour once famously, perceptively, wittily and woundingly observed, 'has written another book about himself. Only this time, he has called it *The World Crisis*'.

The result was that, for much of his adult life, Churchill's attitude to formal education at all levels was not only deeply ambivalent but also fascinatingly equivocal.[16] As far as the general population was concerned, he was no zealot in favour of mass schooling. He certainly recognised there should be an elite who ought to be better educated than he had been, but he was never in favour of extending this privilege to the majority of the young population, whom he once revealingly described as attending 'village schools with a few half-naked children rolling in the dust'. While Chancellor of the Exchequer from 1924 to 1929, Churchill did all he could to cut spending on state schools in the pursuit of retrenchment and economy, so much so that the president of the board of education, Lord Eustace Percy, was convinced that he was taking belated personal revenge for his own unhappy schooldays.[17] Churchill's revealing response was to dismiss the hapless and beleaguered minister as 'Lord Useless Percy'. During the Second World War, R. A. Butler was in charge of education for much of the time, and although he never suffered as Percy had, he concluded that the prime minister's interest in the subject was 'short, intermittent and decidedly idiosyncratic'. Churchill did not regard the post as 'a central job', and he thought the purpose of mass education was to 'tell the children that Wolfe won Quebec'.[18] Nor did his opinions on the subject mellow with age: as peacetime premier between 1951 and 1955, Churchill paid scant attention to Florence Horsbrugh, the minister of education, whom he regarded as a

---

[15] *MEL*, p. 378; D. Cannadine, *In Churchill's Shadow: Confronting the Past in Modern Britain* (2003), pp. 89–90.
[16] A. Montague Browne, *Long Sunset: Memoirs of Winston Churchill's Last Private Secretary* (1995), pp. 264–65.
[17] Lord Eustace Percy, *Some Memories* (1958), p. 96.
[18] Lord Butler, *The Art of the Possible* (1971), pp. 90, 108; P. Addison, *Churchill on the Home Front, 1900–1955* (1992), pp. 363–64.

weak and marginal figure *and thus an appropriate person for the job*, and he did not initially give her a seat in cabinet; while his private opinion was that the recently-raised school leaving age should be lowered back to fourteen.[19]

As for universities: in his own case, Churchill could never quite decide whether missing out on higher education at Oxford or Cambridge had been a grave disadvantage, because his mind had never been challenged and trained and disciplined by serious teaching and demanding learning; or whether he had had a lucky escape from the parochial shackles of academic pedantry and the arid constraints of scholarly obscurantism, leaving his mind free to range untrammelled, uninhibited and unintimidated across many areas of human knowledge. Put another way, this meant he was uncertain as to whether he was disappointed or reassured that figures such as Plato and Aristotle, to say nothing of the ancient Romans, had had the temerity to anticipate some of his own later ideas.[20] And in any case, the army itself had been a formative experience for him during late adolescence and early adulthood – albeit within limits. Regimental life in India, he recalled, 'was a grand school for anyone. Discipline and comradeship were the lessons it taught; and perhaps after all they were just as valuable as the lore of the universities. Still, one would like to have [had] both'.[21] As for those who were allegedly studying: Churchill increasingly felt that university life was so important that it was often wasted on the young; and he came to 'pity undergraduates, when I see what frivolous lives many of them lead in the midst of precious, fleeting opportunity'. Indeed, if he had had his way, he would have made what he termed 'drastic changes in the education of the sons of well-to-do citizens':

> When they are sixteen or seventeen, they begin to learn a craft, and to do healthy manual labour, with plenty of poetry, songs, dancing, drill and gymnastics in their spare time. It is only when they are really thirsty for knowledge, longing to hear about things, that I would let them go to university. It would be a favour, a coveted privilege, only to be given to those who had either proved their worth in the factory or field, or whose qualities and zeal were pre-eminent.[22]

As these vivid but varied quotations from *My Early Life* make plain, there was a sort of insecure yet rather belligerent uncertainty in Churchill's general attitude to the higher learning. Beyond any doubt, he possessed a mind,

---

[19] D. Cannadine, J. Keating and N. Sheldon, *The Right Kind of History: Teaching the Past in Twentieth-Century England* (2011), pp. 107–8; *Speeches*, viii. 8293.
[20] Lady V. Bonham Carter, *Winston Churchill As I Knew Him* (1967 edn.), pp. 18–19; *MEL*, p. 37.
[21] *MEL*, p. 225.
[22] *MEL*, p. 127.

albeit largely untrained, of remarkable force, range, breadth, originality and creativity. As Sir Kenneth Clark, who was not easily over-awed, and who knew Churchill quite well, once put it, in response to a BBC interviewer who suggested he was no intellectual: 'Don't be taken in. He was a man of a wonderful and very powerful mind'. But as Lord Eustace Percy observed, Churchill was also impatient and disdainful, as a self-educated man, of those who had been taught by more rigid, formal and structured means.[23] This may help explain his lifelong dislike of middle-class intellectuals such as Professor Harold Laski, and he was always deeply hostile to the notion of government by experts. (His close friendship with Professor Frederick Lindemann was very much the exception that proved the rule.) And just as there was always a touch of Etanswill about Churchill's politics, so there was always a hint of philistinism about his (undeniably large and varied) hinterland. Although he was an accomplished painter, he loathed modern art; he was fascinated by science, but this was derived from his youthful reading of Jules Verne and H. G. Wells; his taste in music never advanced beyond the popular songs of his late Victorian youth and the works of Gilbert and Sullivan; and his historical inspirations were Gibbon and Macaulay rather than Marx and Weber.[24] All of which is but another way of saying that universities and the intelligentsia were far from being Churchill's obvious spiritual homes or soul-mates. Neither professors nor undergraduates were his natural friends: the former might be appropriate as scientific advisors or research assistants, but otherwise he had a generally 'low opinion' of them; the latter were all too often pampered and privileged drones, and this was very much what his own wayward son Randolph would be during his four terms as an undergraduate at Christ Church, Oxford.[25]

Not surprisingly, then, during the first half-century of his life, Churchill's connections with higher education had been virtually non-existent: he had been elected Rector of Aberdeen University in 1914, but because his term of office coincided almost exactly with the First World War, he neither spoke at nor visited the place, and he would not do so until he received an honorary degree in 1946.[26] Yet a decade on, at almost just the time he was

---

[23] BBC Radio London, 27 August 1976: Kenneth Clark interview with Roger Clark. I am grateful to James Stourton for this reference. Percy, *Some Memories*, p. 97.

[24] Cannadine, *In Churchill's Shadow*, p. 112; J. H. Plumb, 'The Historian', in A. J. P. Taylor et al., *Churchill: Four Faces and the Man* (Harmondsworth, 1969), p. 127.

[25] Montague Browne, *Long Sunset*, p. 265.

[26] W. D. Simpson, *The Fusion of 1860: a Record of the Centenary Celebrations and a History of the United University of Aberdeen, 1860–1960* (Edinburgh, 1963), p. 39; CHAR 13/44/126, Sir George Adam Smith to WSC, 7 November 1914; University of Aberdeen, Special Collections, MS 2913: WSC to Sir George Adam Smith, 10 November 1914; *Speeches*, vii. 7306–8.

setting down his ambivalent thoughts on higher education in *My Early Life*, he was appointed Chancellor of the University of Bristol. How could this possibly have happened? What claims did this under-educated, aristocratic autodidact have on any British university, let alone Bristol? In truth, he had scarcely any; and by the late 1920s, Churchill was also someone whose political star was distinctly on the wane. By 1929, he had been in public life for thirty years, and while even his most incorrigible enemies conceded that he possessed elements of greatness and genius, it was also widely believed that he was a man of unstable temperament and wayward judgement, as evidenced by his lengthening catalogue of mistakes and misfortunes, among them Tonypandy, Sidney Street, Antwerp, the Dardanelles, Chanack, the return to the Gold Standard and his conduct during the recent General Strike. Moreover, his stately, mannered, ornate, and essentially nineteenth-century oratorical style seemed increasingly out of date in the era of the wireless, the Bright Young Things and Lytton Strachey's debunking of those allegedly *Eminent Victorians*. Not for nothing would Robert Rhodes James call his pioneering investigation of Churchill during these years *A Study in Failure*.[27] Having once been regarded as a young man with a brilliant future before him, Winston Churchill was increasingly seen by the late 1920s as an old man with a brilliant future behind him. Why, then, at this low point in his career, and with no significant claim on any British university, did Bristol decide to select him as its Chancellor?

---

[27] Cannadine, *In Churchill's Shadow*, pp. 97–8, 101–2; R. Rhodes James, *Churchill: A Study in Failure, 1900–39* (1970), p.121.

2. Appointed Chancellor

By the end of the 1920s, the University of Bristol had been in existence for less than a quarter of a century, having received its royal charter only in 1909. When Churchill was invited to become its Chancellor, the entire undergraduate body numbered slightly less than one thousand, but Bristol could boast some above-averagely fine buildings. As such, it was one of several English, provincial, red-brick universities that had been founded during the early years of the twentieth century, the others being Liverpool, Manchester, Leeds, Sheffield and Birmingham. All of them were established on the basis of local initiative and with start-up funds provided by wealthy industrialists: the ship-owners and chemical manufacturers in Liverpool, the cotton-ocracy in Manchester, the master cutlers in Sheffield, and so on. To this, Bristol was no exception, for the majority of its early funding came from the Fry family, who had made their money in chocolate, and (even more) from the extended Wills dynasty who had accumulated their several fortunes in cigarette manufacturing.[1] But although these new universities were appropriately established with new money, most of them tended, when it came to selecting their chancellors, to go for traditional aristocratic figures with local territorial connections, and this pattern would last until the Second World War and beyond. There were successive dukes of Devonshire at Leeds, and earls of Derby at Liverpool; and the duke of Norfolk, the marquess of Crewe and the earl of Harewood formed an aristocratic trio at Sheffield. Indeed, there were only two exceptions to this general trend of electing coroneted chancellors. One of them was Birmingham, where Joseph Chamberlain was both the city's political boss, and the driving force behind the establishment of the university. He thus became its founding chancellor, and after his death, Birmingham never turned to a local, landowning aristocrat when filling that office.[2]

The second exception to this general rule among England's provincial universities was Bristol. As with Joseph Chamberlain at Birmingham, the founding chancellor was not a local landed grandee: instead he was a resident businessman and philanthropist, Henry Overton Wills III, whose major benefaction of £100,000 (perhaps £10 million in today's values) had

---

[1] H. E. Meller, *Leisure and the Changing City, 1870–1914* (1976), pp. 91–5; M. Sanderson, *The Universities and British Industry, 1850–1970* (1972), pp. 71–3.

[2] D. Cannadine, *Lords and Landlords: The Aristocracy and the Towns, 1774–1967* (Leicester, 1980), pp. 56–8; D. Cannadine, *The Decline and Fall of the British Aristocracy* (1990), pp. 573–8, 720–2.

Figure 3. Dr. Thomas Loveday, Vice Chancellor, 1922–44.

been essential in getting the fledgling university off the ground. But Wills died in 1911 after only a very brief tenure, and in his memory his sons, Henry Wills and George Wills, would give further substantial sums to construct a fine memorial building, opened in 1925.[3] Wills was succeeded by a very different sort of chancellor, Lord Haldane. Once again, he was no aristocratic potentate with local territorial connections; but unlike Wills, he was a lawyer and philosopher, who had been educated in Britain and Germany, and who had been a Liberal MP and had served as Secretary of State for War from 1905 to 1912, when he drove through overdue and important reforms of the army. From 1912 until 1915, Haldane was lord chancellor, but he was forced to resign because of his supposed (but unproven) German sympathies. Thereafter, he moved to the left in politics, and again served as Lord Chancellor in the first Labour government of 1924. Haldane was not only a major public figure, but also an authentic scholar-statesman and cosmopolitan intellectual, who was a Fellow of the British Academy and a member of the Order of Merit. He also cared deeply about education, and played a major part in the establishment of the London School of Economics and of Imperial College. But beyond these impressive achievements and appropriate qualifications, Haldane's particular appeal to Bristol was that he had given crucial strategic advice to the University's founding fathers during the 1900s; and throughout his term of office, he continued to be closely involved in Bristol's affairs, bringing King George V and Queen Mary down to open the Wills Memorial Building in 1925.[4]

When Haldane died, in August 1928, there was thus no precedent for approaching a local grandee to be the University's senior officer. The first two Chancellors had been very different figures, and also very different from each other: a Bristol businessman and princely benefactor, and a major politician with a profound interest in education. Unlike Wills, Churchill was not rich, and he had no significant local ties to Bristol; unlike Lord Haldane, he had never been associated in the popular imagination or the professorial mind with higher education; and although he had undoubtedly been a major figure in public life for almost three decades, the general view was that he was unstable, unreliable and was in all likelihood a spent force. How, then, did Churchill's name emerge? It was initially proposed by Sir William McCormick, a former professor of English literature at University

---

[3] A. M. Tyndall, 'A University in Bristol', in *Bristol and its Adjoining Counties*, ed. C. M. McInnes and W. F. Whittard (Bristol, 1955), pp. 327–30; *Bristol*, pp. 21–23, 29–39; F. M. L. Thompson, *Gentrification and the Enterprise Culture: Britain, 1780–1980* (Oxford, 2001), pp. 55, 63, 89, 170, 174, 176, 178–79.

[4] E. Ashby and M. Anderson, *Portrait of Haldane at Work on Education* (1974), pp. 63, 89, 92–3, 149–50, 155–6; *Bristol*, pp. 15–19, 129–32.

College Dundee, and the first Secretary of the Carnegie Trust for Scottish Universities, who later became a renowned academic administrator. He had been closely involved with Lord Haldane in the creation of the University Grants Committee (UGC), of which he became first chairman in 1919, and he held that post until his death eleven years later. The UGC was responsible for disbursing the money made available to British universities from the Treasury, which meant McCormick was directly responsible to the Chancellor of the Exchequer, and this was how he came to know Churchill, who held that office throughout Baldwin's government of 1924–29.[5] The Chancellor and the chairman clearly got on, and in 1925, McCormick helped persuade Churchill to restore government funding to universities to the level it had been before the post-war cuts of 1921. When urging Churchill's claims to the Bristol Chancellorship, McCormick may have shown astonishing prescience: 'If you want to get the aid of the man whose name will live in English history', he is alleged to have said, 'invite Winston Churchill'.[6]

Churchill's candidacy was taken up by two senior Bristol figures who could also claim personal and political connections with him: Thomas Loveday, the Vice-Chancellor, and Henry Hobhouse, the Pro-Chancellor. Loveday was descended from an old Oxfordshire family, was a country gentleman with an estate in the county at Williamscott, and had been Vice-Chancellor since 1922, having previously been Principal of University College, Southampton. Moreover, Loveday's uncle, James Cheape, of Strathtyrum, Fife, was married to an aunt of Clementine Churchill's; and this family connection would later ease the formality of the meetings between Chancellor and Vice-Chancellor. Henry Hobhouse was an even grander figure: the scion of a major Somerset landowning family, he had been Liberal MP for a local constituency from 1885 until 1906, which meant he had overlapped with Churchill in the Commons; and his kinsman Charles Hobhouse had sat with him in Asquith's cabinet. It was Loveday who had sought McCormick's advice, which he had good reasons for welcoming; and he also canvassed John Buchan, the recently elected MP for the Combined Scottish Universities, who likewise recommended Churchill.[7] While these consultations were being undertaken, there was a general

---

[5] G. C. Moodie, 'Buffer, coupling and brake: reflections on sixty years of the University Grants Committee', *Higher Education*, xii (1983), 332–3; M. Shattock and R. Berdahl, 'The British University Grants Committee, 1919–83: changing relations with government and the universities', *Higher Education*, xiii (1984), 472.

[6] *Bristol*, pp. 37, 98; UoBSC DM 1053: notes by Sarah Markham.

[7] UoBSC DM 1058: Sarah Markham, Reminiscences of TTL, March 1977, p. 1; *Burke's Landed Gentry* (17th edn., 1952), pp. 1570–71; *Bristol*, p. 50.

election at the end of May 1929, and the Conservatives were turned out and a minority Labour government took office instead. This abrupt transition from power to opposition may have further diminished Churchill's appeal, and there was clearly some unease in the University about the proposed appointment. A committee had been set up by Council, the 'executive body of the University', in October 1928, to oversee the nomination of a new Chancellor. The minutes reveal little of the discussions that went on, but its proceedings were delayed by disagreement, and it was only in June 1929, and after a hostile amendment was defeated, that Council was able to forward Churchill's nomination for Chancellor to the Court, which was the University's 'supreme governing body'.[8]

The recommendation of the University Council was duly ratified by the University Court, and the Vice-Chancellor, the Pro-Chancellor and the Chairman of the Court then delivered the formal invitation to Churchill in person. His first response was 'to be excused from accepting on the grounds that his claims to an academic appointment were insufficient'; but his understandable hesitations and serious doubts were overborne, and he was installed as Chancellor in mid December 1929, in a succession of events that were an appropriate combination of the informal and the ceremonial, the disruptive and the carefully arranged.[9] After a boisterous reception at Temple Meads railway station by the undergraduates, Churchill's installation took place in the Great Hall of the Wills Memorial Building, after which he conferred honorary degrees on the poet Walter de la Mare, the composer Ralph Vaughan Williams, Admiral Sir Roger Keyes, and the educationalist (and Bristol graduate) Thomas Franklin Sibley. Also honoured were three politicians: Walter Runciman, who had been a ministerial colleague of Churchill's in his Liberal phase; Margaret Bondfield, who as Minister of Labour in Ramsay MacDonald's government of 1929 had become the first woman to join the cabinet; and her colleague Philip Snowden, who had recently succeeded Churchill as the Chancellor of the Exchequer (Neville Chamberlain should also have attended, to provide cross-party balance, but he was abroad). There followed a dinner for the honorary graduands and such local dignitaries as the Lord Mayor, the Bishop and the Sheriff of Bristol; the next evening Churchill and Clementine attended a reception for two thousand guests; and the new Chancellor also appeared at the Territorial Army Ball, opened the Wills Hall of Residence and declared

---

[8] UoBSC DM 1143: Minutes of University Council, 18 December 1928 to 4 June 1929; DM 219, 'The Government of the UoB' [c1945], pp. 1–2.

[9] UoBSC DM 1571: PRM, recollections of WSC, 22 July 1953, pp. 1–2; CHAR 2/168, TTL to WSC, 27, 29 June 1929, 22 November 1929; WSC to TTL, 29 June 1929, 14, 19 November 1929.

it 'the finest hostel in the Empire', was 'captured' and 'fined' as part of a student 'rag', and addressed the assembled undergraduates at the University Union.[10]

This was one of several speeches that Churchill made during his inaugural visit. After his installation, he paid tribute to his 'old friend and colleague', Lord Haldane; he hoped that the University might become a new 'focus and centre-point upon which local patriotism and endeavours' might be concentrated; and he urged the cause of higher education as 'the surest way to reconcile the past with the present… to build the causeway to our future'. At the dinner that evening, Churchill spoke warmly of Henry Hobhouse and of the honorary graduates, and noted that as Chancellor he exercised general authority over the University, but 'had yet to ascertain the full extent of his powers and duties'. (Loveday later told Churchill that his powers were both 'everything and nothing'.)[11] But it was Churchill's speech to the undergraduates that was his most carefully-prepared and revealing. 'I never', he began, 'had myself the opportunity of a university education. I was not thought clever enough to profit by its advantages'. Accordingly, when he 'began to read and wanted to know about a lot of things', he had 'nobody to tell me about them', and he had 'found myself ever since at a great disadvantage' compared to those who had been better educated. 'I wonder', he went on, 'if you appreciate how lucky you are, how much the gift of education has been valued and counted by those to whom it has been denied'. Here were thoughts and arguments that he was setting out more fully in *My Early Life* at just this time. Churchill then turned to offer some unexceptional advice, encouragement and exhortation: he believed an appetite for education mattered; he thought that learning should be lifelong; and he warned that both love and sorrow were an inescapable part of the human condition. 'This young new generation', he concluded, had been lucky enough to avoid the carnage of the First World War: but, 'just as you have great responsibilities, so you have great opportunities'.[12]

This may have been how things looked, in late 1929, to Bristol's new Chancellor and to the University's most recent cohort of graduates, when the transatlantic impact of the Wall Street Crash in New York was nothing like as severe as it would later become, when the good-time boom of the 1920s still seemed in full roll and abundant momentum in western Europe, and

---

[10] UoBSC DM1462/1/1–2: UoB, Installation of the…Chancellor of the University, 13 December 1929; Dinner in the University, 13 December 1929; Evening Reception, 14 December 1929; DM 1430, Wills Hall Opening Ceremony, 14 December 1929.

[11] *Bristol Evening News*, 13 December 1929; *Times and Mirror*, 14 December 1929.

[12] *Sunday Times*, 15 December 1929; *Western Daily Press*, 16 December 1929; CHAR 9/88 A-B, WSC, drafts of UoB speech.

Figure 4. Churchill borne shoulder-high by undergraduates on his first visit to Bristol as Chancellor, December 1929.

when the 'challenges' and 'responsibilities' facing the University of Bristol's new graduates might indeed be balanced by possibilities and opportunities. But during the next few years, as the Wall Street Crash morphed into the global Great Depression, the 'opportunities' of which Churchill had spoken at the time of his installation would rapidly diminish and effectively disappear, which meant that for many young people, Bristol graduates included, the 1930s would offer little prospect except unemployment for most of the decade, followed by compulsory wartime military service at the very end of it. Thus regarded, 1929 was not only a significant and conjoined year in Churchill's biography and in the history of the University of Bristol: it was also the year in which the attempt to put the clock back to the pre-1914 world of European and global stability, based on the Gold Standard, was effectively given up.[13] Although he could not have known it at the time, Churchill was not only assuming the Chancellorship of the University when his own political career seemed to be winding down: he was also taking it on as one of the most dismal and disorienting decades of the twentieth century

[13] P. F. Clarke, 'Churchill's economic ideas, 1900–30', in *Churchill*, ed. R. Blake and W. R. Louis (New York, 1993), p. 95.

was about to begin. During the 1930s, he would himself become ever more politically adrift and so, too, would much of Europe and the Far East; and in addition to continuing to extol the benefits of a university education, Churchill's speeches at Bristol during the 1930s would increasingly reflect on and regret these broader contemporary developments and, as he saw them, significant and ominous deteriorations.

The ceremonials of December 1929 were wholly without precedent, for Churchill was the first Chancellor of the University of Bristol to be installed in the Great Hall of the Wills Memorial Building. It had only been completed four years before his appointment, and the large, majestic central space had been deliberately planned for the holding of examinations and for the staging of major events. The whole complex was designed as one of the last great secular works of the Gothic Revival, and as a lifelong habitué of the Palace of Westminster, the new Chancellor must have felt immediately at home amidst its armorial shields, its delicate tracery, its stained glass windows and its vaulted ceilings.[14] But this was not the only way in which Churchill's Chancellorship differed from that of his two predecessors. Wills and Haldane had both performed their ceremonial duties wearing a robe that had been specifically designed and made for the exclusive use of the University's most senior officer. But uniquely among Bristol's Chancellors, Churchill was able to provide his own, equally appropriate attire. Since the eighteenth century, Chancellors of the Exchequer had, on ceremonial occasions, worn a robe made of black silk trimmed with gold, resembling those worn by the Lord Chancellor and the Speaker of the House of Commons. In 1853, and against all precedent, the outgoing Chancellor, Benjamin Disraeli, had refused to relinquish the robe to his rival and successor, Mr. Gladstone; and when Lord Randolph Churchill was briefly Chancellor of the Exchequer in 1886, he had purchased his own robe, which Lady Randolph kept 'in tissue paper and camphor' for forty years after his death.[15] When Stanley Baldwin offered her son the same post in 1924, Winston Churchill replied: 'this fulfils my ambition. I still have my father's robes as Chancellor. I shall be proud to serve you in this splendid office'.[16] While at the Exchequer, he was drawn wearing his Chancellor's robe by John Singer Sargent; and having relinquished that post, but having become another sort of Chancellor, Churchill resolved to wear the same robe on ceremonial occasions at the University of Bristol, which he duly did from his installation onwards, assisted by a page to carry what he called his 'tail'.[17]

[14] B. Cottle and J. W. Sherborne, *The Life of a University* (Bristol, 1959 edn.), pp. 44–55; *Bristol*, pp. 127–32.
[15] R. Blake, *Disraeli* (1966), pp. 350–2; H. Pelling, *Winston Churchill* (1974), p. 298.
[16] *C&G*, v. 59.
[17] UoBSC DM 1058: Sarah Markham, Reminiscences of TTL, March 1977, p. 1.

Appointed Chancellor

The years 1929–30 were not only the time when Churchill became Chancellor of Bristol, and wrote *My Early Life*, with its extended and equivocal ruminations on the merits and drawbacks of higher education: they also coincided with his only son Randolph's unhappy and wasted terms at Oxford, which caused him to ponder further the point and purpose of advanced learning. Like his grandfather, but unlike his father, Randolph had attended Eton, but he left early in order to begin his studies at Christ Church in January 1929. Churchill's friendly scientist, Professor Frederick Lindemann, who was a Student (ie Fellow), had helped ensure Randolph obtained a place, but he showed less interest in work than in drinking and socialising and talking. By the end of the year, Randolph was determined to leave Oxford with no degree; but as Roy Harrod, another Student, would later recall, Winston tried hard to dissuade him:

> He discoursed on the nature of a university, and on the merits of a university education. He spoke of the ripe judgement and the mellow wisdom of university teachers. They had devoted their lives to reading, studying and reflection. They were unique in this respect. Through their teaching one could learn to be a wiser man. Then he talked about his own experience, in a modest and charming way, about how his lack of university education had handicapped him in his political career, about how, in the cut and thrust of debate with someone like Arthur Balfour, he had felt himself at a disadvantage for lack of the weapons that a university education could have given him. It was the most splendid eulogy of the university function.

But, Harrod went on, 'I was watching Randolph during Winston's discourse. It was all flowing over him, so it seemed to me, like water off a duck's back'.[18] After just four terms, and to his father's great annoyance and disappointment, Randolph dropped out of Oxford, thereby passing up the educational opportunity Winston would always regret he had never had – a regret that his recent elevation to the Chancellorship of Bristol, and his happy encounter with the University's undergraduates and senior staff at his installation, may well have reinforced.

---

[18] W. S. Churchill, *His Father's Son: The Life of Randolph Churchill* (1996), p. 70; B. Roberts, *Randolph: A Study of Churchill's Son* (1984), pp. 39–41, 83.

3. Apprentice Chancellor

Having been installed and inaugurated as Bristol's third Chancellor, Churchill would, as was then the rule, hold the office for life, and by the time he died in 1965 he would be by some margin the longest-serving senior officer of any British university.[1] But in terms of his public career, the 1930s were not an easy decade for him, and there was no indication that Sir William McCormick's confident prediction of a golden future for Churchill would be borne out any time soon, if, indeed, ever. The Labour Party disliked him for the belligerent part he had played in the General Strike, for describing them as being 'unfit to govern', and for his increasingly intransigent stance as a 'class warrior'. Many Conservatives had never trusted him since he had defected to the Liberals early in his political career; the long campaign he waged from 1929 to 1935 against the Government of India Bill made him new enemies in the Party; his later warnings against the growing Nazi menace went largely unheeded as a result; his support of King Edward VIII at the time of the abdication seemed further evidence that his judgement was almost invariably faulty; and by then he was so disliked and distrusted that in the winter of 1938–9 he came close to being de-selected by his constituency association in Epping.[2] Thus regarded, Churchill was at best an unreliable maverick, at worst a diehard and embittered extremist, increasingly out of touch with the tone and the temper of the times. Indeed, *My Early Life* was in many ways a nostalgic lament for what its author increasingly saw as the vanished but much better world of his youth, when Britannia ruled the waves, when the British Empire seemed unchallenged, when the Gold Standard regulated international finance, and when Free Trade seemed an article of faith. At two other British universities, which had sent him invitations to speak soon after Bristol had asked him to be Chancellor, he made the first of several speeches in which he lamented what he saw as the deteriorated state of mass democracy and of parliamentary government in Britain, initially in his Romanes Lecture at Oxford in June 1930, and then in his Rectorial address at Edinburgh in May the following year.[3]

---

[1] UoBSC DM 219: 'The Government of the UoB' [*c.*1945], p. 1.
[2] P. Addison, *Churchill: The Unexpected Hero* (Oxford, 2005), p. 151.
[3] WSC, *Parliamentary Government and the Economic Problem* (Oxford, 1930); CHAR 2/169/35: J. S. Allan to WSC, 30 May 1930; CHAR 9/95/145–163: WSC, text of University of Edinburgh Rectorial Address, 5 March 1931; P. Addison, *Churchill on the Home Front, 1900–1955* (1992), pp. 287–315.

For the remainder of the 1930s, no other universities in Britain paid Churchill any serious attention, but during his wilderness years, Bristol stood by him, and this constancy when he was increasingly isolated and disoriented was something for which he would remain abidingly grateful. Yet it took time for the relationship between him and them to settle down, and for Churchill to find his feet in what was for him at the outset a largely alien world. Moreover, his chaotically busy life meant that on several occasions he abruptly withdrew from Bristol engagements, not yet realising that University events and ceremonials required a long lead time in terms of planning, preparation and the sending out of invitations, which meant that they could not be easily rearranged or cancelled at short notice. In the summer of 1933, for example, celebrations were planned to mark the hundredth anniversary of the Bristol organisation that was the precursor of the University's medical school. All the arrangements were in place and the date was fixed for 1 July, which would coincide with the general congregation at which degrees would be awarded to those who had just graduated, and Churchill agreed to appear. But in mid June, he accepted a subsequent and more pressing invitation to make 'an important speech' in France on that date, and had to cancel Bristol. The Vice-Chancellor expressed his disappointment at the Chancellor's absence, but gamely undertook to stand in for him.[4] Later that year, Churchill agreed to attend another degree ceremony which would be held in October to inaugurate the University's law school, and at the Vice-Chancellor's behest, he persuaded the Lord Chancellor, Lord Sankey, to come down to accept an honorary degree. Once again, all seemed fixed, but then Churchill had to pull out to attend the Conservative Party Conference, and since the date could not be altered, the ceremonies for a second time went ahead without him, with the Vice-Chancellor again regretting Churchill's withdrawal.[5]

The conclusion that the University authorities rightly drew from these awkward episodes was that asking Churchill down for such particular events was not a good idea. On the other hand, he was clearly eager to attend honorary degree ceremonies, and the general congregations for new graduates, the more so if the two ceremonials coincided; and it had been thanks to his intervention and invitations and that Snowden, Runciman

---

[4] CHAR 2/184: TTL to WSC, 22, 28 November 1932; WSC to TTL, 25 November 1932; CHAR 2/202: TTL to WSC, 15, 16 May 1933, 11 June 1933; V. Pearman to TTL, 19 May 1933; WSC to TTL, 10 June 1933.

[5] CHAR 2/202: TTL to WSC, 12, 28 June, 5, 6, 19 July, 16, 29 August 1933; WSC to TTL, 14 June, 12 August 1933; WSC to Lord Sankey, 29 June 1933; Lord Sankey to WSC, 3 July 1933.

and Keyes had all accepted honorary degrees at the time of his installation.[6] In June 1931, Churchill presided for the first time as Chancellor over the general degree congregation, and at the end of it he also conferred honorary doctorates on the Reverend Archibald Henry Sayce (a Bristol-born archaeologist and sometime professor of Assyriology at Oxford), Hiatt Cowles Baker (Pro-Chancellor of the University and Master of the Society of Merchant Venturers), and Neville Chamberlain (minister of health in the Conservative Government of 1924–29), whom Churchill had initially invited to be present at his installation, but who had been out of the country at the time.[7] In the two-and-a-half years that had elapsed since then, the global economic situation had dramatically deteriorated, and Churchill had paid two extended visits to the United States; and after congratulating the graduates and the honorary graduates, his comments as Chancellor reflected both these changed circumstances and his own recent travels. He lamented that it was now 'impossible for millions of workers on both sides of the Atlantic to earn their daily bread', he regretted that 'Germany has been reduced to desperate straits', he applauded President Hoover's decision 'to proclaim and enforce a general moratorium for a year in the payment of war debts and indemnities', and he rejoiced that Britain had followed America's lead. 'A willing association', he concluded, 'of the English-speaking peoples in all parts of the globe in a policy of revival and easement is the brightest augury for the future, and a sure guarantee that the day will not be far distant when the hands of industry and the powers of science will once again be rewarded with a sense of active progress in an age of peace and plenty'.[8]

Churchill's second appearance in Bristol at a full degree congregation was in June 1935. The honorary graduates selected by the University Council were Field Marshal Sir William Birdwood (formerly Commander-in-Chief of the Indian Army, Master of Peterhouse, Cambridge, and an Old Cliftonian), Sir Malcolm Hailey (former Governor of the Punjab and of the United Provinces), and Sir Charles Grant Robertson (Vice-Chancellor of Birmingham University). The names of Anthony Eden, who was a rising star in the Conservative Party, and George Forbes, the prime minister of New Zealand, had also been proposed, but neither could attend. Churchill suggested Lord Hugh Cecil and Lord Lloyd instead, on the grounds that

[6] CHAR 2/168: WSC to TTL, 28 July 1929.
[7] UoBSC DM 1462/4/xiii: TTL to WSC, 24 February 1931; DM 2331/4–6: N.Chamberlain to D. Badcock, 12 May 1931, 23 June 1931; DM 1736/1: UoB, Degree Congregation of June 27th 1931.
[8] *Times and Mirror*, 26, 29 June 1931.

they would 'add to the distinction and catholicity' of the list.[9] But Cecil was notorious for his incorrigibly belligerent Anglicanism, while Lloyd had been one of Churchill's strongest die-hard supporters in his recent, protracted and futile campaign against the Government of India Act. Moreover, the University Council, which was responsible for deciding on the honorary graduates, would not be meeting again before the degrees were due to be conferred. 'It would', the Chairman of Council tactfully but firmly explained to the Chancellor,

> obviate a great deal of inconvenience and not a little criticism of our procedure if you would allow us to defer consideration of these other names until some future year. We look forward with keen anticipation to repeated visits from you in the future. May I hope for your concurrence in this view of the matter? We desire to show due deference to your wishes as Chancellor, but you will see how acute our immediate difficulty is.

'I have no wish', Churchill replied, 'to put you to any inconvenience, and naturally comply with your wishes'. But he also asked to be consulted 'before the next batch of honorary degrees is decided upon, in case I have any suggestions to make which might be helpful and pleasing to the University'.[10]

The degree ceremony duly took place, 'with a blaze of colour of the gowns of the various faculties, centring on the gorgeous robe of gold and black' of the Chancellor himself; but neither the economic nor the international situation had improved since Churchill's previous visit, four years earlier.[11] Indeed, the whole period of his Chancellorship, he told his listeners, had thus far witnessed 'very grave changes', which amounted to nothing less than the 'melancholy retrogression of civilisations in many of the greatest countries in the world'. Nations were becoming 'walled off from each other by ever increasing barriers against trade and intercourse', which meant that 'the hideous problem of unemployment' remained unsolved, and that there had been 'utter failure to make any successful progress towards the harmonious combination of the forces of production and consumption'. But in addition, he went on, 'we have seen law and justice, the principles of freedom, the rights of the individual as against the state', all 'those great pillars of civilisation', being 'increasingly disregarded over large parts of

---

[9] UoBSC DM 1516/5: TTL to WSC, 1 February 1935; CHAR 2/250: TTL to WSC, 17, 28 May 1935; WSC to TTL, 20 May 1935.
[10] CHAR 2/169/21: TTL to WSC, 17 February 1930; CHAR 2/250, S. H. Badcock to WSC, 24 May 1935; WSC to S. H. Badcock, 25 May 1935.
[11] UoBSC DM 1516/5: UoB, Degree Congregation of June 29th 1935.

Europe'. In far too many nations of the world, there was 'a retreat from all those broad platforms of civilisation gained in the great Liberal epoch of the nineteenth century'. By contrast, in Britain the privations and misfortunes of the depression were being withstood better than in many other countries, and the laws and liberties of the land remained intact. But the young men and women who had just graduated would be going out to face a dangerous and hostile world; they had a 'high and noble duty' to preserve Britain's 'precious heritage' for future generations; and for that they would need all 'the qualities of foresight, earnestness and resolution' which had 'long distinguished the citizens of Bristol'. If such challenges could be met with such character, he hoped that 'we shall not find the storms of the future greater than those through which our forbears navigated their barque'.[12]

Throughout his time as an active Chancellor, Churchill's speeches would always reflect his current political preoccupations, and this sort of jeremiad, with an exhortatory conclusion added on, became his rhetorical stock in trade during the 1930s. The next few years would be his most difficult politically, and although they were never acrimonious, his relations with the University of Bristol again seem to have been slightly strained. Once Anthony Eden had become foreign secretary at the end of 1935, it proved impossible to find a time when both he and Churchill could be in Bristol together, and during the next two years, several dates were fixed for the conferring of his postponed honorary degree, only to be cancelled by one or other of them at short notice.[13] Churchill was also surprised to learn that no honorary degrees would be awarded in 1937, and asked for the matter to be reconsidered. 'It is an advantage to the University', he informed the Vice-Chancellor, 'to add a few distinguished friends to their supporters at these Congregations, and it invests the annual ceremony with additional significance'. But Loveday held firm: it was impossible to change the arrangements at this stage, and in any case, the University's general principle was 'to award honorary degrees about once in three years'. This was the usual practice outside Oxford and Cambridge, and there were special reasons for adhering to it in Bristol, for when Haldane had been installed as Chancellor in 1912, the University had awarded *seventy* honorary degrees, and this 'injudicious prodigality' meant that ever since it had given

---

[12] *Bristol Evening Post*, 29 June 1935; *Western Daily Press*, 1 July 1935.
[13] CHAR 2/250: TTL to WSC, 28 November 1935, 11 December 1935; WSC to A. Eden, 8 December 1935; A.Eden to WSC, 13 December 1935; CHAR 2/291, TTL to WSC, 4 May 1936; WSC to TTL, 9 May 1936; A.Eden to WSC, 25 June 1936; CHAR 2/323, TTL to WSC, 23 April 1937, 6 May 1937; WSC to A. Eden, 26 April 1937; WSC to TTL, 7 May 1937.

them out very sparingly.[14] Honorary degrees would be awarded again in 1938, but this time, the Senate and Council decided that 'any such degrees should on this occasion be confined to persons distinguished in academic life or in letters, science or art'. Churchill was understandably annoyed at not having been consulted, as he had earlier requested, and Loveday, clearly embarrassed, hastened to mollify him: sometimes universities 'extended their hospitality widely' in conferring honorary degrees (as Bristol had done three years ago); but on other occasions they restricted themselves ('as we are doing this year').[15]

Churchill once again declined to press his point, but it seems unlikely that he was exhilarated by the slate of savants with which he was presented: the poet T. S. Eliot, the physicist Charles Galton Darwin, and the archaeologist Mortimer Wheeler, along with the former Medical Officer of Health in Somerset and the professor of international relations at Oxford. The good news was that Anthony Eden would also be able to attend, and Churchill duly conferred six honorary degrees in early July 1938, the third time he had done so at a general congregation.[16] The bad news was that only four months before, Hitler had absorbed Austria into the German Reich, and Churchill was in an even more sombre mood than he had been in 1935, as he spoke again of the values and the vulnerabilities of the European way of life. 'The central principle of civilisation', he began, was 'the subordination of the ruling authority to the settled customs of the people, and to their will as expressed through the Constitution'. Britain today, he went on, had 'achieved in a high degree the blessings of civilisation. There is freedom; there is law; there is love of country; there is a great measure of goodwill between classes; there is a widening prosperity'. But in the 'turbulent, formidable world outside our shores', the picture was far darker, and 'declarations of right principles' would count for nothing 'unless they are supported by those qualities of civic virtue and manly courage and by those instruments and agencies of force and science which in the last resort must be the defence of right and reason'. And so to his Gibbonian climax:

---

[14] CHAR 2/323: WSC to TTL, 26 April 1937; TTL to WSC, 28 April 1937; *Bristol*, pp. 28–29. The fashion for awarding honorary degrees in large numbers seems to have been established by Lord Curzon at Oxford in 1907: M. Hall, *George Frederick Bodley and the Later Gothic Revival in Britain and America* (2014), pp. 1–2; D. Cannadine, *Aspects of Aristocracy: Grandeur and Decline in Modern Britain* (1994), p. 99.

[15] CHAR 2/352: W.Shapland to Members of Council and Senate, 4 February 1938; WSC to TTL, 7, 11 February 1938; TTL to WSC, 9 February 1938.

[16] CHAR 2/352: TTL to WSC, 18 March 1938, 21 June 1938; WSC to TTL, 28 March 1938, 27 April 1938; WSC to A. Eden, 27 April 1938.

> Civilisation will not last, freedom will not survive, peace will not be kept, unless a very large majority of mankind unite together to defend those ideals, and show themselves possessed of a constabulary power before which barbaric or atavistic forces would stand in proper awe.[17]

'Here, then, we see', he concluded, addressing those who had just graduated,

> the task which should command the generous exertions of the rising generation, which fills this spacious hall, and which may bring to the life of Britain a surge of the new impulse towards the organization of world peace, and across the gulf of these eventful years bring nearer the brotherhood of man.[18]

This was the last general degree congregation over which Churchill would preside as Bristol's Chancellor, and just three months later, at the end of September 1938, the Munich Agreement was negotiated, whereby Hitler effectively obtained control over Czechoslovakia. Amidst the ever-darkening European scene, when another war against Germany seemed increasingly unavoidable, and when he was more insistently but vainly urging the cause of Anglo-American co-operation, Churchill brought Joseph P. Kennedy, the American ambassador, down to Bristol in May 1939 to receive an honorary degree. In personal terms, their relationship was not an easy one. In the autumn of 1933, Kennedy had visited Britain, and with the impending end of Prohibition, had sought to obtain the franchise to ship scotch and other liquor to the United States. Churchill may have helped open some doors for him in London, and Kennedy would eventually make millions of dollars from the deals he was able to conclude. At the same time, Churchill had also received substantial amounts of stock in two American companies controlled by Kennedy. Two years later, Kennedy visited Britain again, and Churchill's American friend, Bernard Baruch, urged him to see Kennedy 'as he is important and good relationships between you might have far-reaching results'.[19] So, indeed, they might have, but although Kennedy visited Churchill at Chartwell, close ties between them were never satisfactorily established, and by the time Kennedy arrived in Britain as Ambassador

---

[17] R. Quinault, 'Winston Churchill and Gibbon', in *Edward Gibbon and Empire*, ed. D. McKitterick and R. Quinault (Cambridge, 1997), pp. 317–22; D. Cannadine, *The Undivided Past: Humanity Beyond Our Differences* (New York, 2013), pp. 219, 229–30.

[18] *Speeches*, vi. 5990–91; CHUR 9/132: WSC, UoB Speech, 2 July 1938; *The Times*, 4 July 1938; *Western Daily Press*, 4 July 1938.

[19] CHAR 2/237: B. Baruch to WSC, 25 September 1935; WSC to Joseph P. Kennedy, 27 September 1935; CHAR 1/272/113: Joseph P. Kennedy to WSC, 27 December 1935; D. Nasaw, *The Patriarch: The Remarkable Life and Turbulent Times of Joseph P. Kennedy* (New York, 2012), pp. 191–4, 238–9; T. Maier, *When Lions Roar: The Churchills and the Kennedys* (New York, 2014), pp. 83–95.

early in 1938, the two men were well on the way to taking up irreconcilably opposing positions regarding Britain's attitude to Germany. Churchill loathed the policy of appeasement, thought war with Hitler would come, that Britain must prepare for it, fight it and, with American help, win it. Kennedy feared that a European conflict would spell the end of capitalism as he knew it, and as he had profited from it, that Britain probably would not fight Germany and certainly would not win, that appeasement was thus the only possible policy, and that the United States should stay out of any future European war. Hence his strong support for Neville Chamberlain and his growing disagreement with Churchill, whom he increasingly came to dislike and to distrust.[20]

Yet hoping against hope, Churchill invited Joseph P. Kennedy to Bristol to receive an honorary degree, in what was clearly one last attempt to win him over. After all, Bristol had strong Anglo-American associations: it was the city from which Sebastian Cabot had ventured forth to the new world, and from which Isambard Kingdom Brunel's *Great Western* had set out to cross the Atlantic. But by the spring of 1939, the international scene was even darker than it had been when Churchill had last been at the University: 'the great antagonisms in the world', he noted in his speech at a dinner that evening honouring Kennedy, 'are moving steadily forward. Europe is more than two thirds mobilized tonight'. To be sure, there was no cause for the British people to suppose that 'the United States was going to come and fight their battles' for them. But he was equally certain that 'there is no good future for the world if Great Britain and America are divided, and there is no better hope for the future of the world than that it shall be founded upon the ever-increasing companionship and friendship…[and] unity between the great English-speaking peoples of the world'. Kennedy's reply was distinctly lukewarm, praising Churchill for his oratory, thanking him for the degree he had conferred, and telling some jokes, but he offered little encouragement or support for the Chancellor's grandiose Anglo-American vision. From Churchill's perspective, the Ambassador's visit was not a success, and by the summer relations between them would have deteriorated still further; but as his warnings about Nazi Germany seemed increasingly vindicated by recent events, Churchill's own political stock was steadily rising, and in welcoming him to the dinner, the University of Bristol's Pro-Chancellor offered another prediction as to how posterity might soon come to view him:

[20] *C&G*, v, 1074–75; A. Smith (ed.), *Hostage to Fortune: The Letters of Joseph P. Kennedy* (New York, 2001), pp. 229–34; J. S. Rofe, 'Joseph P. Kennedy, 1938–40', in *The Embassy in Grosvenor Square: American Ambassadors to the United Kingdom, 1938–2008*, ed. A. R. Holmes and J. S. Rofe (2012), pp. 27–8; Maier, *When Lions Roar*, pp. 132–6, 144–6, 177–90

In years to come students of history will find few greater contributions to the strength and safety of this country than the courageous and constructive criticism and the great qualities of statesmanship which he has displayed in the critical times through which we have been passing.[21]

---

[21] N. Nicolson (ed.), *Harold Nicolson: Diaries and Letters, 1930–39* (1966), p. 403; *Western Daily Press*, 26 May 1939; *Bristol Evening Post*, 25 May 1939.

4. Wartime Chancellor

Within a few months, Britain was indeed at war with Germany, and Churchill had been proven right in his persistent warnings about the evil nature and predatory intentions of Nazi Germany. At the commencement of hostilities, he was summoned back to power as First Lord of the Admiralty, and in April 1940 he succeeded Neville Chamberlain as prime minister. Joseph P. Kennedy did not think Churchill was up to the job, and despite the premier's magnificently defiant speeches, he remained convinced that Britain faced certain defeat at the hands of Nazi Germany, and that the United States should stay out of the war. But Kennedy could not have been more wrong: for during the next five years, Sir William McCormick's prediction that Churchill would make a name that would 'live in history' would be triumphantly vindicated, as he stormed his way to greatness and talked his way to glory.[1] He would also be an unrelentingly busy man during these stern and stirring years, but he did not forget Bristol or its University. Among the members of his wartime coalition government who were drawn from the Labour party were two men with strong local connections: Ernest Bevin, his Minister of Labour, who had worked in Bristol as a young man, and had begun his career there as a trades union official; and A. V. Alexander, the First Lord of the Admiralty, who had been born in Bristol and grown up in the nearby holiday resort of Weston-super-Mare. During the first full year of the war, Bristol was subjected to very heavy German air raids, and Bevin kept Churchill in touch with how its citizens were coping with the blitz. Thus informed, he wrote to the Lord Mayor in December 1940: 'my thoughts have been much with the inhabitants of Bristol in the ordeal of these last weeks'. As Chancellor of the University, he went on, 'I feel myself united to them with a special bond of sympathy, and I have heard with pride of the courage, resolution and patience with which they have answered these detestable attacks on their families and their homes'. Later that month, the University was hit, and the Great Hall of the Wills Memorial Building was badly damaged; and Churchill wrote to the Vice-Chancellor, expressing his sorrow and sympathy, and also his relief that the destruction was less than it might have been.[2]

---

[1] D. Nasaw, *The Patriarch: The Remarkable Life and Turbulent Times of Joseph P. Kennedy* (New York, 2012), pp. 427–43; J. S. Rofe, 'Joseph P. Kennedy, 1938–40', in *The Embassy in Grosvenor Square: American Ambassadors to the United Kingdom, 1938–2008*, ed. A. R. Holmes and J. S. Rofe (2012), pp. 32–42; N. Rose, *Churchill: An Unruly Life* (1994), pp. 263–70.

[2] CHAR 20/2A-B: WSC to E. Bevin, 10 December 1940; WSC to the Lord Mayor of Bristol, 10 December 1940; WSC to TTL, 13 December 1940.

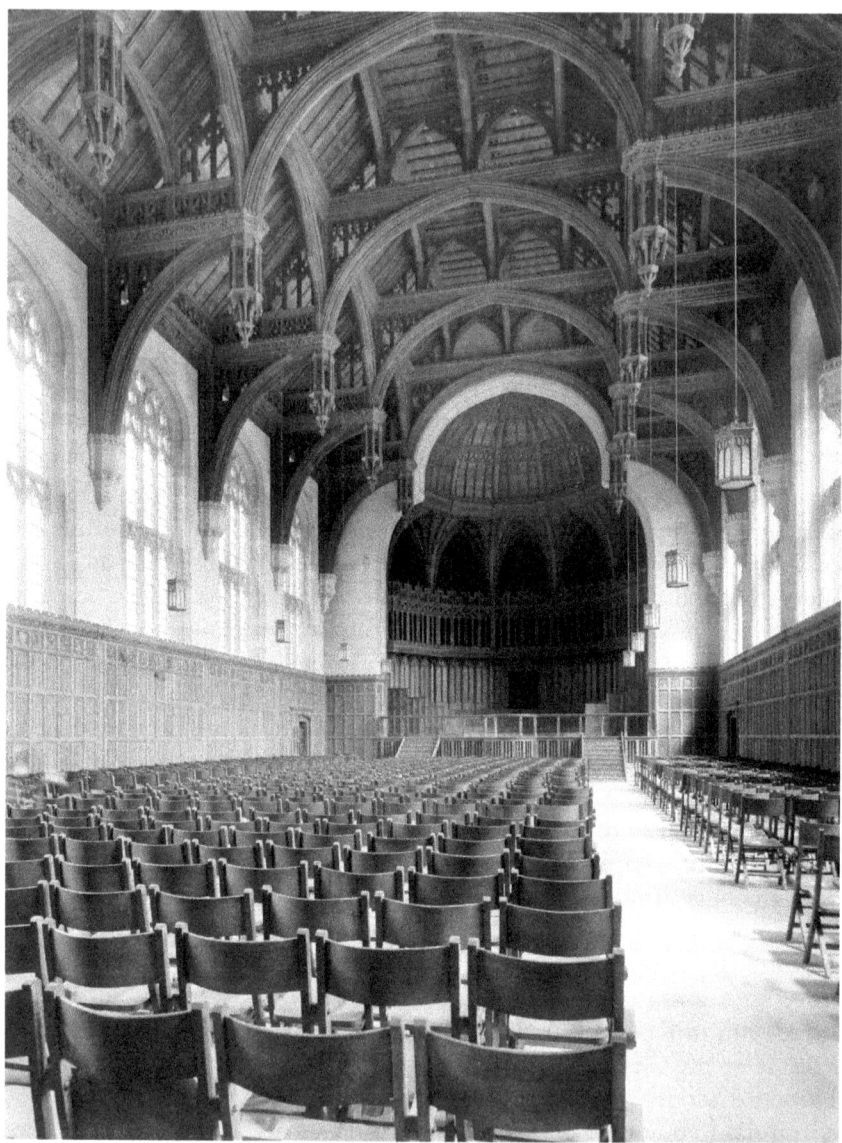
Figure 5. The Great Hall of the Wills Memorial Building before bomb damage.

Figure 6. The Great Hall after bomb damage in December 1940.

By this time, and under growing pressure from the Roosevelt administration, Joseph P. Kennedy had resigned as American Ambassador and returned to the United States, and Churchill found his strongly pro-British successor, John Gilbert ('Gil') Winant, much more congenial.³ In the early spring of 1941, it so happened that Robert Menzies, the prime minister of Australia, and James Bryant Conant, the President of Harvard University, were both visiting Britain, and Churchill conceived the idea of giving them, and the new Ambassador, honorary degrees at Bristol. It would also be an opportunity for him to show the three men how a provincial city was enduring the German air raids, to thank a representative of one of the great dominions for their contribution to the war effort, and in the aftermath of the recent passing of the Lend-Lease Bill by the US Congress, to celebrate the cause of Anglo-American amity and urge still greater co-operation. The University had not planned to hold any honorary degree ceremonies for the duration of the war, but at Churchill's suggestion, it willingly extended invitations to Conant, Menzies and Winant, and amidst strict security measures the visit to Bristol was scheduled to take place in early April, on Easter Saturday.⁴ The day before, Conant had been compelled to return to the United States, and he would be awarded his honorary degree *in absentia*; and the night before, Bristol was subjected to one of the most savage and sustained air raids of the entire war. When Churchill reached the City the following morning, much of it lay in ruins: two hundred people had been killed and twice as many were injured. Among his party was one of his private secretaries, the young Jock Colville, who described it as a scene of 'devastation such as I had never thought possible'. Churchill toured the city, accompanied by the Lord Mayor, and he was visibly moved by the crowds of people who gathered to cheer him as the news of his visit spread. He inspected the damage, talked with some of the victims of the raid, and shook hands with civil defence workers, many of whom had been in action for twelve hours without a break. 'God bless you all,' he told them, 'we will give it to them back'.⁵

At the University, where 'the gowns and pageantry were a strange

---

³ Nasaw, *The Patriarch*, pp. 480–86; A. Smith (ed.), *Hostage to Fortune: The Letters of Joseph P. Kennedy* (New York, 2001), pp. 475–77; L. Olson, *Citizens of London: The Americans Who Stood with Britain in its Darkest, Finest Hour* (New York, 2010), pp. 24–6, 69–71; D. Mayers, 'John Gilbert Winant, 1941–46', in *The Embassy in Grosvenor Square: American Ambassadors to the United Kingdom, 1938–2008*, ed. A. R. Holmes and J. S. Rofe (2012), pp. 51–5.

⁴ CHAR 2/432A-B: TTL to Commander Thompson, 2, 3, 8, 9 April 1941.

⁵ J.R.Colville, *The Fringes of Power: Downing Street Diaries, 1939–1955* (2004), p. 322; *Bristol Evening Post*, 12 April 1941; *Oxford Mail*, 12 April 1941; *Sunday Times*, 13 April 1941; *Western Daily Press*, 14 April 1941.

Figure 7. The Chancellor with Robert Menzies and Gil Winant, having conferred honorary degrees on them, April 1941

contrast to the smoking ruins just outside', Thomas Loveday welcomed the Chancellor 'on this your first visit to us since you resumed high office' and saluted the 'eloquence and example' of his wartime leadership; and he expressed his delight that two distinguished figures from different parts of 'the English-speaking world' were being honoured. 'Our buildings are scarred and mutilated', he concluded; 'our ceremonial hall is in ruins; our company is small. But you find your University undaunted in an undaunted city, its spirit high, its temper resolute'.[6] Some professors arrived late, their faces stained and grimy, and wearing their academic robes over their still-wet fire fighting clothes. After conferring degrees on Menzies and Winant, and having spoken of them in fulsome terms, Churchill went on to tell his audience: 'That we should be assembled here, and gathered here in this way, is such a mark of fortitude and phlegm, of a courage and detachment from

---

[6] Colville, *Fringes of Power*, p. 322; CHAR 2/432A-B: text of TTL's speech enclosed with TTL to Commander Thompson, 8 April 1941; *Western Daily Press*, 14 April 1941.

material affairs worthy of all that we have learned to believe of ancient Rome or of modern Greece'.[7] Churchill, Menzies, Winant and the senior officers of the University then went outside and were greeted with loud cheers. At the end of the visit, as his train pulled out of Bristol station, one of the prime minister's party noticed that his eyes were filled with tears, and he picked up a newspaper to hide his face. It was an occasion that Churchill never forgot: he invariably mentioned it on his subsequent visits as Chancellor, and when he received an honorary degree at Harvard University from President James Conant two years later, he began his speech by recalling the 'faultless ritual and appropriate decorum' that he had witnessed in Bristol on that April day amid so much death, devastation and ruin. 'I sustained', he went on, 'a very strong and invigorated impression of the superiority of man over the forces that can destroy him'.[8]

For as long as there were people who could remember, that wartime visit of Churchill's to the beleaguered University and to the blitzed and bombed-out city of Bristol created a bond with him that would last until the end of his life. He had stood with them, and been among them, in the darkest of hours and the hardest of times.[9] But as so often with Churchill, and especially during his years of supreme power, he was operating at many different levels, and he had many different agendas, and the defiant pageantry of that Bristol degree ceremony was no exception. During the early months of 1941, the war was not going well for Britain: in north Africa and the Balkans, the German advance seemed inexorable, while the still hard-fought and undecided Battle of the Atlantic remained a source of constant anxiety, and the support for the British provided by the United States remained far below that which Churchill sought, and which would be essential if Britain was to defeat Hitler rather than merely survive. These were the worries that lay behind the resolute pose that Churchill struck at Bristol, and there were personal tensions, too, with his guests. The new American Ambassador, Gil Winant, was much more pro-British than his predecessor, and was eager to mend fences; but that was no guarantee that the United States would come into the war on Britain's side, and like Roosevelt, he was no admirer of the British Empire.[10] James G. Conant was another strong supporter of Britain in its fight against Hitler, but as the

---

[7] *Speeches*, vi 6377–78.
[8] *C&G*, vi. 1058–59; M. Gilbert, *Churchill and America* (2005), pp. 218–21; M. Soames, *A Daughter's Tale: The Memoir of Winston and Clementine Churchill's Youngest Child* (2011), pp. 192–93; *Sunday Times*, 14 April 1941; *Western Daily Press*, 14 April 1941; *Manchester Guardian*, 14 April 1941; *The Times*, 14 April 1941; *Speeches*, vii. p. 6823.
[9] UoBSC DM 1143: UoB, Minutes of Council, July 1964–July 1965, p. 106.
[10] Mayers, 'John Gilbert Winant, 1941–46', pp. 57–58.

man who presided over the Manhattan project, he was also determined that the development of the atomic bomb would be an exclusively American undertaking, from which he wanted the British excluded.[11] As for Robert Menzies: he had come to Britain as a fierce critic of Churchill's, for his failure to send British forces to safeguard Australia in the event of a Japanese invasion; he was highly sceptical of many aspects of the prime minister's style of leadership; and he may even have harboured ambitions to supplant him as the supreme director of the British Empire's war effort.[12] So behind the publicly united façade of the Bristol degree ceremony, matters were nothing like as consensual as they seemed.

But there was yet a third layer of meaning and significance to this wartime ceremonial amidst the still-smouldering ruins of the city and the University. For as Churchill had no doubt hoped and intended, Gil Winant was greatly impressed by the bravery and fortitude of the citizens of Bristol, and so was Averell Harriman, President Roosevelt's Special Envoy, who was also present. Winant reported to Roosevelt that Churchill received a great reception, despite 'the strain and nightmare of the recent hours', and Harriman was so moved by the courage of the Bristol people he encountered that he sent a substantial cash gift to Clementine Churchill, asking her to forward it to the Lord Mayor, to help those who had lost their homes. In her note of thanks, Mrs Churchill, taking a leaf out of her husband's book, expressed the hope that 'all this pain and grief... may bring our two countries permanently together and that they may grow to understand each other'. Whatever happens, she concluded, 'we do not feel alone any more'. In many of their subsequent letters and cables to President Roosevelt, Winant and Harriman emphasised not only the resolution, determination and courage of the British people, but also the crucial role that these ordinary men and women were playing in the conflict. As their experience of Bristol (and other cities) constantly reminded them, this was indeed a 'people's war'.[13] Likewise, although Robert Menzies remained both suspicious and critical of Churchill, he, too, presented a gift to the men and women of Bristol, in the form of a mobile canteen donated by the Australian Mutual Provident Society. He was also genuinely overwhelmed by the courage of ordinary people who were enduring ordeals that had been completely beyond his imagining before his arrival from Australia; and later

---

[11] J. G. Hershberg, *James B. Conant: Harvard to Hiroshima and the Making of the Nuclear Age* (New York, 1993), pp. 143–46, 191–93; G. Farmelo, *Churchill's Bomb: A Hidden History of Science, War and Politics* (2013), pp. 173–5, 224–6.

[12] But cf Menzies' very different recollections of his relationship with WSC in R. G. Menzies, *Afternoon Light: Some Memories of Men and Events* (1967), pp. 44–5, 62–94.

[13] Olson, *Citizens of London*, pp. 79–81.

that year, Menzies would publish a book of the speeches he had delivered on his recent visits to Britain's battered and wounded towns and cities, including that which he gave in Bristol on that April day.[14]

Soon after his Bristol expedition, Churchill wrote to the Vice-Chancellor 'both as prime minister and as Chancellor of Bristol University', proposing to recommend him for a knighthood. 'I know', he noted, 'that this suggestion has been made to you before and that you did not wish your name to be included in the list'. But he hoped that Loveday might now 'see your way clear to accepting this recognition of the distinguished services you have rendered the University'. 'Your words of friendliness and confidence', the Vice-Chancellor replied, 'have given me great pleasure', but 'with regret', he felt compelled again to decline 'a suggestion honourable in itself and doubly gratifying because it comes from you'. In the past, he had 'openly expressed a doubt of the suitability of equestrian rank as a recognition of the services of academic persons', and he could not 'alter my attitude' now.[15] Two years later, in May 1944, Loveday announced he would retire from the Vice-Chancellorship the following September, having been invited to undertake educational work for the Ministry of Agriculture. Churchill sent a gracious letter, acknowledging the great debt that the University owed him for his 'long and distinguished Vice-Chancellorship', and thanking him for 'your constant help to me as Chancellor'. 'It has fallen to my lot to hold many public offices', he concluded, with perhaps a touch of exaggeration, 'but I cannot recollect one in which my relations with those in authority have been characterized by such ease or felicity'.[16] The University set about finding 'a young and vigorous Vice-Chancellor', and Churchill was kept fully informed. The preferred candidate was Oliver Franks, who had been born in Bristol and attended the local grammar school; after being educated and then teaching at Oxford, he had been appointed professor of philosophy at the University of Glasgow, and had enjoyed a meteoric rise as a wartime civil servant in the Ministry of Supply. But in peacetime, Franks preferred to return to the Queen's College, Oxford, as Provost, and instead Bristol appointed Sir Philip Morris as the next Vice-Chancellor; he had been previously director of education in Kent and the wartime director-general of army education, and he would serve for

---

[14] A. W. Martin and P. Hardy (eds.), *Dark and Harrowing Days: Menzies' 1941 Diary* (Canberra, 1993), p. III; R. G. Menzies, *To the People of Britain at War* (1941), pp. 81–82.

[15] CHAR 20/21A-C: WSC to TTL, 24 May 1941; CHAR 2/520A-B, TTL to WSC, 26 May 1941.

[16] CHAR 2/520A-B: TTL to WSC, 14 May 1944; WSC to TTL [draft, 30 May 1944].

Figure 8. Churchill receiving the Freedom of Bristol at the Council Chambers, April 1945.

twenty years, retiring the year after Churchill's death.[17]

Although the University authorities would have been delighted to host another such morale-boosting wartime visit, Churchill did not appear again in Bristol until April 1945, when hostilities in Europe were almost over.[18] It was a day of double ceremonial, for the prime minister was also given the Freedom of the City, which he had accepted two years earlier, and this time there was no need for secrecy.[19] Bells pealed, flags waved and crowds cheered

---

[17] CHAR 2/520A-B: Sir S. H. Badcock to WSC, 11 May 1944; WSC to Sir S. H. Badcock, 31 May 1944; UoBSC DM 2331/2–11: WSC to Sir S. H. Badcock, 19 March 1945; *Bristol*, pp. 51–53.
[18] CHAR 2/455A-B: TTL to WSC, 24 March 1942.
[19] CHAR 2/484A-B: L.A.Parish to A Bevir, 24 August 1943.

Figure 9. The Chancellor with Ernest Bevin and A. V. Alexander, having conferred honorary degrees on them, April 1945.

as Churchill made his triumphant way in the City's semi-state coach from Temple Meads Station to the Council House, accompanied by the Lord Mayor, the duke of Beaufort and the City Sword-bearer. 'In giving him the freedom of the city', the *Western Daily Press* opined, 'Bristol applauds the man of action and the great national leader who has done more than any one man to save not only his country but civilisation itself'. Having signed the roll of honorary freemen in the Council Chamber, where two hundred people had assembled, Churchill wished for 'a period of prosperity to refresh the strong life of the City'.[20] Later, at the University, he bestowed honorary degrees on Ernest Bevin and A. V. Alexander, the two men with strong local connections, but with very different party political affiliations from his own,

[20] *Bristol Evening Post*, 12 April 1945; *Western Daily Press*, 21 April 1945; *Bristol Evening World*, 21 April 1945.

who had served in his coalition government throughout the war. 'I could never have got through this business', he told the assembled congregation, 'if I had not had with me a powerful band of men representative of the nation and bound together by a loyalty which rose far above party politics'. On that occasion, Churchill seemed tired and a little sad, and the impending break-up of the coalition, and the vexing problems presented by the final stages of the war in Europe, meant he did not get round to sending a thank-you letter to the Lord Mayor for several weeks. 'I have been slow in writing to you', he began, 'to express my deep appreciation of the warmth of the welcome given to me'. He ended: 'my two visits to Bristol in the war will ever remain linked in my memory, the first in our dark days, and the second on the threshold of victory'.[21]

When Churchill came to write his multi-volume history of the Second World War, he did not give much attention to events in Bristol, and since he had many grander and bigger subjects to cover in his epic narrative, that was scarcely surprising. He did not mention his visit in the spring of 1945, but he did write eloquently and movingly of the air raids from which Bristol had suffered in late 1940, and of the honorary degree ceremony over which he had presided in April the following year.[22] For him, the city of Bristol epitomised the resolve of the British people not to give in to the intimidating and unrelenting bombardments of the Luftwaffe, while its University was the embodiment of those very civilized values for which he believed that Britain, its Empire and Commonwealth were fighting. But in addition, the Second World War meant that Churchill's position in British political culture, and in British popular opinion, was fundamentally transformed. He was no longer disdained as a marginalised, has-been, extremist diehard, or as a class warrior vainly doing battle against the progressive trends of the times. Instead, he had become a figure seemingly above party, as reflected nationally in his leadership of the coalition government and, more locally, in his bestowal of honorary degrees on those two Labour party stalwarts, Bevin and Alexander, during the closing stages of the war. But the University of Bristol had also given Churchill something extra, which would stand him in good stead in the days of his global fame that were to come. Having served for sixteen years as its Chancellor, he now knew something first-hand about higher education, and he had also had ample practice at addressing professors and undergraduates. These experiences would prove invaluable

---

[21] *Speeches*, vii. 7146–9; *Bristol Evening World*, 21 April 1945; *The Times*, 23 April 1945; CHAR 20/194A-B: WSC to the Lord Mayor of Bristol, 10 May 1945; A.Bullock, *The Life and Times of Ernest Bevin*, ii, *Minister of Labour, 1940–1945* (1967), p. 371.

[22] WSC, *The Second World War*, ii, *Their Finest Hour* (New York, 1949), p. 377; iii, *The Grand Alliance* (New York, 1950), pp. 44–5.

when, in the post-war years, the universities of the free world, extending far beyond Bristol and far beyond Britain, clamoured to salute and to acclaim him.[23]

---

[23] *Speeches*, vii. 7249–51, 7283–5, 7302–3, 7306–8, 7323–4, 7744–6, 7820–1.

5. Opposition Chancellor

Within two months of the second wartime gathering at Bristol, Churchill had ceased to be prime minister, following the Conservatives' landslide defeat at the general election. For the next six years, he would be leader of the opposition: not wholly happily, and not always successfully. But the death of Franklin Roosevelt earlier in 1945 also meant that Churchill was the only surviving allied victor in the west, and his rejection by a seemingly ungrateful people in his hour of supreme triumph only added to his legend and to his lustre, as did the publication of his multi-volume war memoirs that began in 1948. In ways, and to an extent that even Sir William McCormick could never have imagined, Churchill had become a global celebrity, and one indication of his transformed reputation was that universities and colleges across Europe and the United States, which had previously ignored or disdained him, now followed in the footsteps of Harvard, and competed do him honour, and to invite him to speak. Three of these post-war campus speeches were among the most influential he delivered in the later stages of his career, as he sought to offer guidance and counsel at the beginning of what would soon be recognised as the Cold War. At Westminster College in Fulton, Missouri, Churchill warned that the growing Communist menace meant that an 'iron curtain' had descended across Europe, and that it was only by strengthening the 'special relationship' between the United Kingdom and the United States that the freedom and security of the west, and of the world, might be safeguarded. At the Massachusetts Institute of Technology, he explored the same theme of Anglo-American amity, but also spoke of the importance of pure and applied science, and of the beneficent impact he hoped it might make during the second half of the twentieth century. And at the University of Zurich, he called for an end to the deep and historic antagonisms between France and Germany, and for the creation of a United States of Europe.[1]

These were the most famous of Churchill's post-war university addresses, and as *ex cathedra* pronouncements on the sorry state of the contemporary world, but which also offered uplifting prescriptions as to how matters might be rectified, they owed much to the speeches in a similar vein that he had delivered at the University of Bristol during the 1930s. Yet for the most part, and again following the precedent of his earlier Bristol addresses, Churchill preferred to make observations on the importance of higher

[1] *Speeches*, vii. 6823–27, 7285–96, 7379–82, 7801–10.

Figure 10. Sir Philip Morris, Vice-Chancellor, 1946–66.

education, which were invariably prefaced by self-deprecating comments about his own lack of scholarly prowess, and his regret at having never attended university himself. 'One might assume', he remarked at the University of Oslo in May 1948, 'from my many university degrees that I am a very erudite man'. But, he went on, 'when I was young, nobody believed that I should become so learned'. He had never, he continued, in familiar refrain, 'had the advantage of a university training, and I must say I was never any use at the examination desk'. As he recognised, it was 'a great privilege to have received a university training, and the more comprehensive such university studies may have been, the better'.[2] And as he explained when being honoured by the University of London later in the same year, this was a privilege that, 'the more widely it is extended, the better for any country'. The duty of the university, he went on, 'is to teach wisdom, not a trade; character, not technicalities'. From one perspective, then, Churchill advocated undergraduate studies as a route to personal fulfilment; but he also saw universities as institutions devoted to the life of the mind and to safeguarding freedom of thought, and thus as essential bastions 'against all encroachments' on human liberty, be they Fascist or Communist. Places of higher learning, Churchill observed in November 1945 at the University of Brussels, stood for 'the free examination of thought and ideas', and they upheld 'traditions of liberty [that] were so firmly rooted that no thoughts of compromise could be entertained'.[3]

Has any other British prime minister, or leader of the opposition, ever spoken so frequently or so eloquently in defence of universities and in praise of the benefits, both individual and collective, of higher education as Churchill did between 1945 and 1955? Or been given, or gladly taken, so many opportunities to do so? But while many universities embraced and acknowledged him in the immediate post-war years, and gave him unprecedented opportunities to speak in high-minded and non-partisan mode, it was with Bristol that Churchill retained and consolidated his one long-term academic connection. He might have seemed to some, himself included, to have been an unexpected and unusual appointment as Chancellor in 1929, with no obvious stature or standing in the world of higher education, and he had taken the best part of the next decade to adjust to and grow into the role; but in the aftermath of the Second World War, Churchill now seemed miraculously reincarnated as a sort of latter-day Renaissance prince, whose unique fame and extraordinary celebrity were appropriately matched by the unrivalled range of his achievements

[2] *Speeches*, vii. 7643–44.
[3] *Speeches*, vii. 7249–50, 7745.

and distinctions. In recognition of his interest in science, he was elected a Fellow of the Royal Society. The amateur artist was made an Honorary [Royal] Academician Extraordinary. The part-time historian and full-time orator was awarded the Nobel Prize for Literature.[4] No other chancellor of a British university ever garnered such an array of academic and artistic laurels, and for someone who had described himself in the pages of *My Early Life* as 'an uneducated man', it was indeed a remarkable tally. Nor did the list end there. King George VI appointed Churchill to be Lord Warden of the Cinque Ports, and bestowed on him the Order of Merit, while Queen Elizabeth II made him a Knight of the Garter, and would have made him a duke had he insisted. Small wonder that Churchill's later visits to the University of Bristol were described as 'royal occasions'.[5]

In the immediate post-war years, and like all of the civic universities founded at the turn of the century, Bristol was about to undergo a period of unprecedented growth that would continue throughout the remainder of Churchill's Chancellorship. Between 1945 and 1965, the University would more than quadruple its pre-war size. At Bristol as elsewhere, this post-war expansion would mainly be financed by the government, via the UGC; but additional residential accommodation was everywhere an urgent priority, as increasing numbers of undergraduates would be living and studying away from home, and to meet this need, private funding was also necessary. Accordingly, in October 1946, the University launched what it called its 'Churchill Appeal', in the belief that 'a very large number of our fellow countrymen, irrespective of political creed, would welcome an opportunity of showing in a practical way their deep appreciation of Mr. Churchill's incomparable leadership during the most critical period in our national history'. The appeal committee, chaired by Herbert Tanner, included local grandees such as Sir Arthur Hobhouse, Lord Bledisloe and the dukes of Somerset and Beaufort, several members of the Wills family, and sundry civic dignitaries, and Churchill himself warmly supported it, providing a handwritten letter which was reproduced in the appeal brochure.[6] The aim

---

[4] D. Cannadine, *Aspects of Aristocracy: Grandeur and Decline in Modern Britain* (1994), pp. 161–2.

[5] UoBSC DM 776: UoB *Gazette*, 'Winston Spencer Churchill, Chancellor of the University of Bristol, 1929–1965' [January 1965], p. 16. Churchill was not the only Lord Warden in modern times who was also chancellor of a university: the same was true before him of Lord Curzon (Oxford), and after him of Sir Robert Menzies (Melbourne) and Queen Elizabeth the Queen Mother (London); but none of them won Nobel Prizes or were members of the Order of Merit.

[6] UoBSC DM 219: The Churchill Appeal for the Extension of the UoB, covering letter by H.G.Tanner; DM 964, UoB, Description of the University's Work and Future… in Connection with the Appeal…to Commemorate the Chancellorship of Mr. Winston Churchill and his Services to the Country and to Humanity [1946].

was to raise £300,000 (perhaps £10 million at today's values), and the appeal met with a generous response not only from Bristol and the West Country, but also from friends and graduates in many parts of the world. Within a year, £250,000 had been donated, the stated target was eventually met, and this financed the construction of Churchill Hall, the first of the new post-war accommodation blocks, which would be opened in 1956.[7]

Meanwhile, Churchill's first peacetime appearance at Bristol had been in June 1946, three months after he had spoken in Fulton. 'Many things have happened since I was last here', he smilingly observed, referring to his electoral drubbing of the year before, 'but one thing at least hasn't changed – I still remain Chancellor of Bristol University'. As in the 1930s, that connection would be a source of strength and support during his second period of rejection and defeat. Global hostilities had ended less than twelve months ago, and in the aftermath of his 'iron curtain' speech there were growing tensions between the west and Communist Russia, so it was scarcely surprising that Churchill's slate of honorands consisted entirely of figures from government and the military: Sir Edward Bridges (Secretary to the Cabinet since 1938), Sir James Grigg (Secretary of State for War from 1942 to 1945), Marshal of the RAF Viscount Portal of Hungerford (Chief of the Air Staff from 1940 to 1945), Admiral of the Fleet Sir James Somerville (scion of a Somerset gentry family, who saw wartime service in the Mediterranean and the Pacific), and the American Lieutenant-General John Clifford Hodges Lee (Commander of US Forces in the Mediterranean Theatre of Operations in Post-War Europe). 'Five or six years of war', Churchill further remarked, 'have slashed across the life of our country and the education of our youth'. The supreme object of a university education, he went on, was to fit men and women to be 'worthy and competent citizens of a free community'. He made the same point when addressing the undergraduates: 'free discussion', he told them, 'is one of the great foundations of a free democracy'. During his visit, Churchill was also made a Freeman of the Society of Merchant Venturers. One of the conditions of acceptance was that all Freemen must refrain from 'the frequenting of taverns and the playing of dice'. But Churchill, whose liking for drink and gambling were well known, had been delighted to discover that such constraints and restrictions in fact applied 'only to apprentices'.[8]

---

[7] UoBSC DM 651: UoB, A report of the appeal made on behalf of the University... to commemorate the Chancellorship of Mr. Winston Churchill and his services to the country and to humanity (October 1946 to March 1948); Cottle and Sherborne, *Life of a University*, p. 135.

[8] *Bristol Evening Post*, 20 June 1946; *Yorkshire Post*, 22 June 1946; *News Chronicle*, 22 June 1946; *Yorkshire Observer*, 22 June 1946; *Daily Sketch*, 22 June 1946; *Glasgow Herald*, 22 June 1946.

Two years later, in July 1948, he was back at the University, but more briefly than on his previous peacetime visit. The sixty executive heads of the universities of the British Empire and Commonwealth were meeting in Bristol that summer; they had not gathered together since before the war, and there was a strong local feeling that Churchill should be present and confer honorary degrees on the President of the University of British Columbia, the Vice-Chancellor of the University of New Zealand, the Principal of the University of Witwatersrand, the Vice-Chancellor of the University of Sydney, the Vice-Chancellor of the University of Ceylon, and the Vice-Chancellor and Rector Magnificus of the University of Malta.[9] Although only recently in post, Bristol's new Vice-Chancellor, Sir Philip Morris, was wholly unintimidated by Churchill's new superstar status, and repeatedly pressed him to appear: 'We are, as I am sure you understand, most anxious that our Chancellor should be with us for some part of the Vice-Chancellors' meeting'. It was, Morris went on, 'exceptionally rare for the Executive Heads of the Universities of the Empire to be assembled together', and he felt this was 'an occasion which you would not wish to miss'. Churchill hesitated, then said no, citing the advice of his doctor, Lord Moran, that he was doing 'too much'; but the Vice-Chancellor was unrelenting in urging that he 'think again', and eventually Churchill agreed, feeling it his 'duty to comply, if physically possible'.[10] He flew to Bristol, stayed for two hours, and then went on to Cardiff, where he was to receive the Freedom of the City. In his speech, after conferring the honorary degrees, Churchill extolled the importance of universities, which 'must realize that even wider and more responsible functions are falling to them than in former times'; of the British Commonwealth and Empire, as 'an institution without parallel in the world', and of a 'united Europe as we hope to see it'. Despite being pressed for time, the occasion was a great success, and Churchill received a warm and rousing reception. 'The Vice-Chancellors of the Universities of the Empire', Morris later told him, 'were unanimous in their gratitude to you and their appreciation of all the trouble you took to come and meet and address them'.[11]

Churchill's post-war visits to Bristol in 1946 and 1948 were indeed Olympian Chancellerial spectacles; but during his years of opposition

---

[9] UoBSC DM 2288/293: UoB, Visit of the Executive Heads of Universities, Congregation for the Conferment of Honorary Degrees by the Chancellor... July 16th 1948.

[10] CHUR 2/302: PRM to WSC, 7 March 1948, 22 May 1948, 31 May 1948, 19 June 1948, 2 July 1948, 13 July 1948; WSC to PRM, 26 May 1948, 30 June 1948.

[11] *Speeches*, vii. 7698–99; *Northern Daily Mail*, 16 July 1948; *Bristol Evening Post*, 16 July 1948; *Bristol Evening World*, 18 July 1948; *Western Daily Press*, 17 July 1948; CHUR 2/302: PRM to WSC, 19 July 1948, 8 November 1948.

Figure 11. The Chancellor with leading figures from the universities of the British Empire and Commonwealth, having conferred honorary degrees on them, July 1948.

from 1945 to 1951, his determination to 'tear their bleeding entrails' out of the Labour Government, and his need to demonstrate to the Conservative rank and file that he was still sufficiently combative and engaged to remain their leader, meant he did not always find it easy – or possible – to reconcile his non-partisan position as a great man and as Chancellor of the University of Bristol with the more pressing demands and imperatives of day-to-day, party political strife.[12] At the next congregation, held in October 1949, he bestowed honorary degrees on Dr. R. W. Moore (formerly headmaster of Bristol Grammar School, but now in charge of Harrow), Professor C. D. Broad (previously professor of philosophy at Bristol, and by then Knightsbridge Professor at Cambridge), Sir Alexander Fleming (the inventor of penicillin), Sir Richard Southwell (the former Rector of Imperial College, London), Field Marshall Viscount Alanbrooke (Chief of the Imperial General Staff for much of the war), and Lewis Douglas (the new American Ambassador to London, to whom Churchill

[12] C. Moran, *Churchill: the Struggle for Survival, 1940–1965* (New York, 1966), p. 335.

was as close as he had been to Winant).¹³ The original list of honorands had been even more distinguished, because it also included Sir Stafford Cripps. He was descended from a family with close links to the region, he represented a Bristol constituency as a Labour MP throughout his time in the Commons, he had been a colleague of Churchill's during his wartime coalition, he had lent his name to the University of Bristol's appeal of 1946, he had succeeded Hugh Dalton as Chancellor of the Exchequer in Attlee's government, and he possessed an unrivalled public reputation for honesty and trustworthiness. Cripps was thus a wholly appropriate figure to be honoured by the University of Bristol, in the tradition of Ernest Bevin and A. V. Alexander; but at the last minute, he withdrew his acceptance, ostensibly on the grounds that 'other engagements made it impossible' for him to attend.¹⁴

Yet the real explanation was rather different. By the late summer of 1949, Britain's post-war economy was in a parlous state, and in September Cripps was compelled to devalue the pound, although in order to prevent a run on sterling he had been obliged to deny until the very last minute that this was what he was going to do. Churchill, whom the Chancellor privately briefed in advance, conceded that it was an unpalatable but brave decision; yet he also warned Cripps that in public, he would 'make the utmost political capital out of it'. And so he did, moving a motion of censure on the government in the Commons for 'four years of financial mismanagement', culminating in devaluation of the pound, which was 'contrary to all the assurances given by the Chancellor of the Exchequer'. While accepting that Cripps's 'personal honour and private character' were 'in no way to be impugned', Churchill insisted that he was 'woefully weakened in reputation', for having 'turned completely round', for having abandoned 'his former convictions', and for doing 'what he repeatedly said he would never do'. How, Churchill asked, pressing his attack remorselessly home, would it be possible for anyone in future to accept with confidence any statements that emanated from the Treasury? This was not how the Chancellor, with all his 'knowledge and integrity', should have behaved.¹⁵ For Churchill, this excoriation was the legitimate small change of party politics; but Cripps took it personally, as a destructive and unfair attack from his wartime leader, in fact impugning his honesty and integrity, even as he denied that he was doing so. Having previously agreed to accept an

---

¹³ UoBSC DM 2288/293: Congregation for the Conferment of Honorary Degrees, 19 October 1949; J. Colman, 'Lewis Williams Douglas, 1947–50', in *Embassy in Grosvenor Square*, ed. Holmes and Rofe, p. 98.

¹⁴ *New York Herald Tribune* (Paris edition), 20 October 1949; *C&G*, viii. 492.

¹⁵ P. Clarke, *The Cripps Version: The Life of Sir Stafford Cripps, 1889–1952* (2002), pp. 520–1; R. Jenkins, *Nine Men of Power* (1974), pp. 102–3; S. Burgess, *Stafford Cripps: A Political Life* (1999), pp. 298–9.

honorary degree at Bristol, Cripps immediately wrote to the Vice-Chancellor withdrawing: 'In view of the Chancellor of Bristol University's observations about myself in the House of Commons last night', he observed, 'it would obviously be impossibly embarrassing for him to have to confer a degree upon me next month'.[16]

In fact, and as their subsequent correspondence makes plain, Churchill felt no embarrassment whatsoever, whereas Cripps, whose health was giving way under the pressure of work, and who was much too thin-skinned for his own good and for the rough-and-tumble of party politics, was both wounded and angry.[17] 'I am sorry indeed', Churchill wrote, on learning of Cripps's withdrawal, 'that you feel my criticism of your political conduct should prevent you from accepting a degree at Bristol University, which it would have given me much pleasure to confer upon you'. He insisted that he had 'in no way impugned' the Chancellor's 'personal honour and private character', and much regretted that the two of them would not now be able to 'meet together on an entirely non-party occasion'. But Cripps remained adamantly mortified: 'I do not', he wrote back, 'wish to receive a degree or any other gift from a person who has publicly accused me of being "void of integrity", "a deceiver", and a liar'. Churchill retorted that he had never used any such words, and that if anyone applied such terms to Cripps, he would 'be among the first to repudiate them'. He hoped that the Chancellor might 'reflect upon these matters in a calmer frame of mind'; but, he went on, in the light of the attitude Cripps had taken, he was 'quite right not to attend our function at Bristol University, much though we shall all regret your absence'. Although not wishing to 'prolong the argument', Cripps sent back a final, brief letter, insisting that the public interpretation of Churchill's words was that he had impugned his honour and integrity. 'I am glad', he concluded, 'at any rate that we agree as to my action as regards the Bristol degree'. The congregation duly went ahead without Cripps; Churchill spoke briefly, deploring the 'ideological wars' between the west and Communism by which the world was vexed, urging the importance of continued close Anglo-American relations, and insisting that 'the intellect of a nation' must 'keep abreast of all material improvements'.[18]

---

[16] CHUR 2/161: Sir Stafford Cripps to PRM, 29 September 1949; Sir Stafford Cripps to WSC, 29 September 1949; PRM to WSC, 30 September, 7 October 1949; WSC to PRM, 8 October 1949.

[17] CHUR 2/161: WSC to Sir Stafford Cripps, 3, 6 October 1949; Sir Stafford Cripps to WSC, 5, 7 October 1949; Burgess, *Cripps*, pp. 299–301.

[18] *Speeches*, vii. 7871–72; *Bristol Evening Post*, 19 October 1949; *New York Herald Tribune* (Paris edition), 20 October 1949; *Southern Daily Echo*, 19 October 1949; *Daily Despatch*, 20 October 1949; *Daily Record and Mail*, 20 October 1949; *Birmingham Gazette*, 20 October 1949; *Western Daily Press*, 20 October 1949.

Heroic Chancellor

Churchill subsequently wrote to the Vice-Chancellor saying how much he and Clementine had enjoyed themselves: 'I think the ceremonies at the University went splendidly', adding, in a clear allusion to the Cripps affair, 'in spite of all!'.[19] But although Churchill remained unrepentant about his swingeing attack on Cripps, and despite his longstanding bewilderment at the Chancellor's punishing personal regime that combined austerity with overwork, his conscience does seem to have been somewhat troubled. They had disagreed about India during the war, but for much of 1942, when Churchill was at his most vulnerable to criticism and attack, Cripps had given him loyal and unswerving support.[20] And although there was a final public spat between them during the general election campaign in February 1950, Cripps remained grateful for Churchill's 'wartime leadership and, indeed, friendship'. Before that year was over, continuing ill health had compelled him to resign as Chancellor and as an MP, and now they no longer crossed swords in the Commons or at the hustings, Churchill hastened to make amends. He sent Cripps a copy of the fourth volume of his war memoirs, which contained a carefully edited account of his mission to India in 1942: 'we have a great story in common', Churchill recalled, 'of those days we went through together'. In November 1951, he renewed his request that Cripps might accept the honorary degree that he had proffered two years before. This time, Cripps accepted, thereby drawing a line under their public feud, although he did not appear in person, but took the degree *in absentia*. 'Clemmie and I send you both our love', Churchill wrote to him, regretting that he could not attend the ceremony. Four months later, Cripps was dead, and Churchill paid him a fulsome Commons tribute, praising his honour and his courage, his abilities and his character.[21]

---

[19] UoBSC DM 1897: WSC to PRM, 3 November 1949.
[20] P. Addison, *Churchill: The Unexpected Hero* (Oxford, 2005), pp. 189–90.
[21] UoBSC DM 1462/1/3: Miss L.M.Marston to PRM, 3 July 1951; PRM to Miss L.M.Marston, 6 July 1951; Clarke, *Cripps Version*, pp. xii, 536–8.

6. Premier Chancellor

By the time Churchill bestowed honorary degrees in December 1951, he had become prime minister again, having narrowly won the general election held two months before. That Bristol congregation had been planned well in advance, while Churchill had still been leader of the opposition, beginning in February, when the Vice-Chancellor had notified Churchill that honorary degrees would again be awarded that year, and expressed the wish that he might be present to confer them on a date to be agreed between them. He hoped that the Chancellor would 'like to make some nominations… when you have had time to consider the matter'; and he was also eager to persuade him to lay the foundation stone of a new building, which would house the Faculty of Engineering and the Departments of Mathematics and Geology.[1] Churchill agreed to all these requests, and for honorary degrees he proposed General Lord Ismay, one of his closest wartime colleagues; Lord Camrose, the press baron who had helped raise the money to buy Chartwell for the nation at the end of the war; James Chuter Ede, who had been Attlee's Home Secretary between 1945 and 1951; Admiral Sir Philip Vian, who had an outstanding war record and was Commander-in-Chief of the Home Fleet; and Sir Philip Morris himself. The Vice-Chancellor took soundings within the University, and concluded that 'on the whole', Churchill's suggestions would 'give rise to no difficulty'. To these, the University added the engineers, A. E. Russell and Sir Charles Lillicrap, respectively the designer of the Brabazon aeroplane (and a Bristol graduate), and the former Director of Naval Construction, and Ralph Vaughan Williams, who had already received an honorary doctorate at the time of Churchill's installation in 1929. But that had been in literature, whereas the recent establishment of 'a full range of musical degrees' in the University meant he could now be more appropriately recognised as Bristol's first honorary Doctor of Music.[2]

During the early summer, the combined list of these nominations made its way from the Committee for Honorary Degrees, via the Senate, to the University Council, and it was duly approved at every stage. The Vice-Chancellor then wrote officially to all the candidates, but in some cases, and as in previous years, Churchill had already sounded them out

---

[1] UoBSC DM 1462/1/3: PRM to WSC, 21 February 1951.
[2] UoBSC DM 1462/1/3: Miss J. Sturdee to PRM, 6 June 1951; PRM to W. R. Verdon Smith, 11 June 1951.

Figure 12. Churchill after addressing students in Colston Hall, November 1954.

informally.³ All seemed settled, when in mid July, Churchill suggested the additional name of the businessman and Conservative MP Sir Ian Fraser, who had been blinded in the trenches during the First World War, and who had devoted much of his later life to charities supporting ex-servicemen who were similarly damaged and disadvantaged. 'As you know', one of Churchill's secretaries wrote to the Vice-Chancellor on his behalf, Fraser had 'given much encouragement to many people by the courageous way in which he faces life under this affliction'. Of course, she went on, 'Mr. Churchill would not wish to press the matter if it is considered that there are already sufficient graduands'; but he would be grateful for advice. 'I think', Sir Philip Morris wrote back with masterly tact, and deploying the same argument that had been deployed in 1935, 'that there are here difficulties which should not be ignored'. Much as he would like to act on Churchill's suggestion, the Vice-Chancellor thought it would be 'a mistake to set aside our traditional way of approving the conferment of honorary degrees'. Since all the appropriate committees had now met and signed off on the agreed list, it was not 'now practicable for approval within the University to be given in the ordinary way' of any additional nominations, and so it would be better to hold Fraser's name over for 'the next opportunity'. Churchill did not force the issue, and did not press his name again; but two years later, and no doubt at his behest, Sir Ian Fraser was instead made a Companion of Honour.⁴

The degree congregation took place on 14 December 1951, and Churchill arrived from 10 Downing Street by train the afternoon before, travelling in a special carriage attached to the London to Bristol express, and accompanied by two policeman, two secretaries and his valet. He was met by the Vice-Chancellor, and escorted to the Royal Hotel, where a secret 'scrambling' device was installed in his suite for the duration of his stay, and where all the newspapers would be delivered to him 'at crack of dawn' the next morning. That evening there was a private dinner for Churchill and the University's guests held at the Society of Merchant Venturers, and the following morning, the Chancellor conferred honorary degrees on the nine nominees, including Sir Stafford Cripps *in absentia*.⁵ In his address to the congregation, Churchill confessed that there was 'no lack of problems for

---

³ UoBSC DM 1462/1/3: Miss L. W. Marston to PRM, 21 June 1951; PRM to Miss L. M. Marston, 23 June 1951.
⁴ UoBSC DM 1462/1/3: Miss L. M. Marston to PRM, 19, 23 July 1951; PRM to Miss L. M. Marston, 20 July 1951.
⁵ UoBSC DM 1462/1/3: Miss J. Sturdee to PRM 5 December 1951; UoB, Congregation for the Conferment of Honorary Degrees and the Laying of the Foundation Stone of the New Engineering School by the Chancellor... 14 December 1951.

Figure 13. The Chancellor laying the foundation stone
of the Queen's Building, December 1951.

the new government to concern itself with', but he also insisted that this was an 'all party occasion'. There were, he noted, fifty million people in Britain, who 'have got to earn their livings and they have got to purchase two fifths of the food they are not able to grow'. But the great advantage the country possessed was its unique, three-fold involvement with the wider world: with the Commonwealth and Empire, with the United States, and with Europe. Once again, Churchill recalled his wartime visit of 1941, and thanked Lord Dulverton (another member of the Wills family) for his donation towards the cost of the restoration of the Wills Memorial Building.[6] Thereafter, he laid the foundation stone of the new engineering block, a task for which he

---

[6] *Evening World*, 13, 14 December 1951; *Bristol Evening Post*, 14 December 1951; *Western Daily Press*, 15 December 1951; *Daily Telegraph*, 15 December 1951.

was particularly well suited, as someone who had laid so many bricks and built so many walls at Chartwell during the 1930s, and who had been 'a member of the bricklayers' trade union for so many years'. 'In the course of laying the foundation stone', Sir Philip Morris later recalled, 'in a way which only he could achieve, he combined frivolous hilarity with real dignity, and so brought about one of those occasions which please all concerned'.[7]

Churchill's peacetime visits to the University of Bristol as prime minister and as Chancellor were classic examples of what might be termed his 'late style' in politics and in public engagement.[8] During the 1930s, when there had been some tensions and disagreements between him and the Vice-Chancellor about the logistics and the business of awarding honorary degrees, and when he himself was politically marginalised and isolated, his manners had been impeccable: he had never in the end gone against the wishes of the University authorities, even when he had clearly disagreed with them; he had always been careful to send his Bristol train bearer a copy of *My Early Life* as a gesture of appreciation; and he had been happy to comply when called upon to put up local university-cum-civic worthies for national honours.[9] Nevertheless, two of his nominations for honorary degrees had been more partisan than consensual, and the University authorities had shown great deftness in fending them off: his suggestions of Lord Hugh Cecil and Lord Lloyd, made in 1935, were never heard of again. But during and after the Second World War, when Churchill acquired a unique national renown and extraordinary global fame, his proposals for honorary degrees were much more broadly based, covering the whole political spectrum, from Conservative to Labour, and although there were some mutterings in the University that academics were insufficiently recognised, the authorities were generally happy to comply with his wishes. From one perspective, it was to Bristol's benefit that Churchill could bring down from London many eminent, distinguished and worldly figures, who would accept an invitation from him but from no one else, and who might become the University's champions and supporters; but it was also another means whereby Churchill could offer recognition and acclaim to friends and colleagues in public life whom he thought appropriately deserving.

Meanwhile, there was one substantive matter that the University had hoped Churchill would take up on their behalf once he was back in power, but on which they would be disappointed. In 1918, the University of Bristol had received its own form of parliamentary representation as its graduates

---

[7] UoBSC DM 1462/1/3: PRM to WSC, 17 December 1951; DM 1571/38, PRM, recollections of WSC, 22 July 1953, p. 5.
[8] E.Said, *On Late Style: Music and Literature against the Grain* (New York, 2006).
[9] CHAR 2/291: TTL to WSC, 4 May 1936; WSC to S. Baldwin, 6 May 1936.

were added to the electorate of the two Combined English Universities seats. But precisely thirty years later the post-war Labour Government abolished the separate university vote and all the university MPs with effect from the next general election, on the grounds that they were an anachronistic and indefensible carry-over from earlier times. The University of Bristol Convocation had unanimously deplored such legislation, and in 1948 conveyed their opinions to Churchill both as Chancellor and as leader of the opposition.[10] The Conservative view, as expressed by Churchill himself several times in Parliament, was that the decision by the Attlee Government to abolish the university seats was a breach of constitutional custom, because it altered the structure of the Commons without the consent of all parties.[11] Moreover, as someone who had grown up in British politics before full adult suffrage had been achieved, Churchill rather liked these lingering remnants of what had once been widespread 'fancy franchises'. In their election manifestos of 1950 and 1951, the Tories accordingly undertook to put back the university seats, and when they were returned to power, the expectation was that they would indeed do so. But since he had only a slim majority, Churchill announced in his first major speech as prime minister that his government would not reinstate the university representation during the life of the new parliament, and in 1955 the Conservatives abandoned the pledge to put back the seats.[12]

Three years after his first peacetime prime ministerial appearance as Chancellor, Churchill celebrated his eightieth birthday in November 1954. There had been nothing like it in British public life since the days of Gladstone, although he had not actually been prime minister at that advanced age, and his espousal of Irish Home Rule made him a much more controversial figure in his later years than Churchill by then generally was. There was an extraordinary outpouring of popular affection and good will towards him, and unprecedented tributes were paid by parliament; but they were marred by the presentation of the Graham Sutherland portrait, to which Churchill and his family took an instant and abiding dislike, and also by some ill-judged remarks about Anglo-American attitudes to Russia during the closing stages of the Second World War, which Churchill had blurted out at a meeting in his Woodford constituency a week before.[13] But in addition, 1954 also marked the twenty-fifth anniversary of Churchill's

---

[10] CHUR 2/302: W. Shapland to WSC, 26 February 1948, enclosing copy of the resolution of the Executive Committee of Convocation.

[11] *Speeches*, vii. 7614, 7618, 7664–65, 7670–71.

[12] *Speeches*, viii. 8291; J. Meisel, *Knowledge and Power: The Parliamentary Representation of the Universities in Britain and the Empire* (Chichester, 2011), pp. 36, 44–46.

[13] *C&G*, viii. 1068–82.

Bristol Chancellorship, and in between the embarrassment of Woodford and the happy but upsetting celebrations at Westminster, he visited the University to confer honorary degrees on Sir Norman Brook (Secretary to the Cabinet), R. A. Butler (Chancellor of the Exchequer), Sir Alan Lascelles (formerly private secretary to King George VI and Queen Elizabeth II), Sir Walter Monckton (Minister of Labour and MP for a Bristol constituency), Sir Hartley Shawcross (Labour's Attorney General from 1945 to 1951), and Herbert Tanner (Treasurer of the University, and the former Chairman of the Churchill Appeal).[14] Taking a welcome break from political controversy and public homage, Churchill again appeared at the University wearing the splendid ceremonial robe that had been made for his father sixty years before. It had been 'most carefully preserved by my mother', he told the assembled University dignitaries, 'until I had the opportunity of wearing it as Chancellor of the Exchequer myself, but also as Chancellor of this University'. And to laughter and applause, he added, 'The alterations which had to be made are really not by any means… fundamental'.[15]

During his visit, Churchill thanked the undergraduates for their birthday gift of an eighteenth-century silver salver, 'on a day', he told them, alluding to the Woodford imbroglio, 'when if you look at the papers, I am supposed to be in a bit of a scrape'.[16] For their part, noted Lord Moran, 'the students had no feeling that he was an old man; on the contrary, he seemed to be one of themselves, and two thousand young voices shouted their joy and approval. The same puckish humour marked his approach to their seniors'. And in his speech to the degree congregation, which he made after entering to music especially composed for his birthday, he linked the anniversary of his installation with the broader currents of public events.[17] 'Today', he observed, was 'nearly as far removed from the Second World War as we were from the Treaty of Versailles on the day I became your Chancellor'. Once again, he went on, Britain had 'regained a large measure of its lost prosperity', and once again, it was 'trying to establish a rule of law for the world under the auspices of most of the great nations'. In the case of developments since 1945, he continued, and unlike those taking place after 1918, 'we have the measureless advantage denied us in the days after the First World War…

---

[14] UoBSC DM 1462/1/6: Elizabeth Gilliatt to PRM, 22 March 1954; UoB, Congregation for the Conferment of Honorary Degrees by the Chancellor, 26 November 1954.

[15] *Speeches*, viii. 8605–07; UoBSC DM 270/2/2–33: Speech by Sir Winston Churchill… at the close of the Congregation for the Conferment of Honorary Degrees, 26 November 1954; *Evening World*, 26 November 1954; *Bristol Evening Post*, 26 November 1954; *The Times*, 26, 27 November 1954; *Western Daily Press*, 27 November 1954.

[16] *C&G*, viii. 1071.

[17] UoBSC DM 1462/1/6: PRM to Lord Dulverton, 30 November 1954.

Figure 14. Churchill conferring an honorary degree on R. A. Butler during his last visit as Chancellor, November 1954.

that the United States is the principal champion and servant and member of the United Nations'. Had that happened, he concluded, at the end of that earlier conflict, 'we might indeed have had a very different story to tell'. Among those present at the congregation was Sir Oliver Franks, who had refused the Bristol Vice-Chancellorship in 1944, and who was also Herbert Tanner's son-in-law. 'I saw [Churchill] at Buckingham Palace a few days before', Franks told Moran, 'sitting on a sofa, apparently too weary to listen to anybody… he seemed a very old man who had not long to live. But at Bristol, he was pink, his expression was full of animation, and his eyes twinkled'.[18]

Some of those attending thought Churchill was less energetic and alert than the comments of Moran and Franks suggested, that he would not long continue in high public office, and that this might be his Bristol swansong. Moreover, he had neither the time nor the energy to sit for the official portrait that the University vainly sought to commission to mark the double anniversary of his eightieth birthday and his silver jubilee as

---

[18] C. Moran, *Churchill: the Struggle for Survival, 1940–1965* (New York, 1966), p. 651.

Chancellor.[19] There was, then, a widespread feeling among those present at Churchill's visit in November 1954 that they might never see him in Bristol again, and that they might have witnessed the beginning of the end of an extraordinary era, both in the history of Britain, and in the history of the University:

> At his last visit, the Chancellor seemed very old. He also seemed blissfully happy. He was then within a few days of his eightieth birthday, yet he attended a special meeting of more than 2,000 undergraduates, and it was with almost boyish delight that he received an unexpected birthday present at the hands of the Lady President of the Union. At the congregation over which he presided, he followed all the proceedings with his usual care, despite increasing deafness; what he said was, as always, essentially simple and human; the wit might sometimes be barbed, but never cynical; as always, he was readily moved to laughter or to tears. Above all, perhaps, he seemed, on this occasion, to be at peace with himself; he had done what he had set out to do. The most dramatic and storm-tossed life of our day was drawing to a triumphant close, amid world-wide affection and esteem. Looking on, we felt that in our lives, too, a chapter was closing.[20]

---

[19] UoBSC DM 1571/21: PRM to WSC, 31 August 1954, 6 October 1954; PRM to Elizabeth Gilliatt, 31 August 1954; WSC to PRM, 26 September 1954.
[20] UoBSC DM 776: UoB, *Gazette*, 'Winston Spencer Churchill, Chancellor of the University of Bristol, 1929–1965' [January 1965], pp. 17–18.

Figure 15. Churchill unveiling a plaque in the Queen's Building, November 1954.

7. Sunset Chancellor

Churchill's visit in November 1954 was indeed his last to the University of Bristol, and during his final decade, he never set foot in the place again. His period as an active Chancellor had come to an end; but it had been a great show, and more than that, while it lasted, and especially during his heroic years beginning in 1940. There had been occasional difficulties, as when two of his nominations were effectively turned down during the mid 1930s, and over Sir Stafford Cripps's refusal to accept an honorary degree in the late 1940s, when Churchill's above-party position as Chancellor was not easily reconciled with his highly partisan role as leader of the Conservative opposition. But he generally showed himself well aware of the limitations of his Chancellerial position, and also of its possibilities, which was why in his years of power and fame he took delight in bringing down public figures from London, thereby giving the University a much higher public profile than would otherwise have been the case. In discharging his tasks, Churchill was also helped by the fact that during his long tenure of office, he only dealt with two Vice-Chancellors, and both Loveday and Morris were men of the highest ability, who handled their Chancellor tactfully but also, when needed, firmly. Above all, and as was to be expected from someone who had always believed that politics and public life were essentially theatrical activities, Churchill *performed* the Bristol Chancellorship brilliantly: before the crowds who cheered him when he stepped down from his train at Temple Meads Station, flourishing a cigar and making the V-sign; in front of the undergraduates who were charmed and flattered to be in the presence of the great man himself; at the honorary degree ceremonies over which he presided with dignity and authority; and in his speeches where he spanned the whole oratorical gamut from stately cadences and torrential eloquence to puckish humour and witty asides. 'Whenever he came to Bristol', Sir Philip Morris later recalled, 'it was particularly delightful to watch his arrival and see him obviously take charge of the place and of its affairs for the short period of his visit'.[1]

Churchill's effective retirement from the Chancellorship, which would be followed a few months after by his departure from the Premiership, ushered in ten sunset years of physical decline and mental decay, made all

---

[1] UoBSC DM 1571/38: PRM, recollections of WSC, 22 July 1953, p. 1; R. Jenkins, 'Churchill: the Government of 1951–55', in *Churchill*, ed. R. Blake and W. R. Louis (New York, 1993), pp. 492–3; J. Rose, *The Literary Churchill: Author, Reader, Actor* (2014), pp. 1–2, 11–14, 448.

Figure 16. Churchill in his Chancellor's robes, painted by Sir Frank Salisbury, *c.*1943.

the harder by his growing conviction that his heroic efforts to preserve the United Kingdom as a great world power had been in vain; but they were also his years of global acclaim and international apotheosis, as he became the object of 'world-wide affection and esteem' that were unique and without precedent. At the University, the Pro-Chancellors or Vice-Chancellor deputised for him on ceremonial occasions, and there were no suggestions that he should resign his office in favour of someone more active and engaged. But the recipients of honorary degrees (which were henceforward awarded annually) were no longer the public figures that Churchill had been able to ask and attract: instead they tended to be local worthies and distinguished academics. In the years immediately after his retirement as prime minister, the Vice-Chancellor still consulted Churchill about nominations; but correspondence on that subject soon lapsed.[2] In 1958, the University secured its first royal visit since that of King George V and Queen Mary a third of a century before, when Queen Elizabeth II agreed to open the new science building bearing her name, of which Churchill had laid the foundation stone seven years earlier. The original plans for the occasion presupposed that Churchill would be present as Chancellor to welcome his sovereign; but by then such events were too physically demanding, and at the eleventh hour, he reluctantly sent his apologies.[3] Thereafter, and at the prompting of the Vice-Chancellor and with the assistance of his private secretary, Anthony Montague Browne, Churchill continued to send letters of encouragement and support, as on the University's fiftieth anniversary in 1959, on the launching of a second appeal three years later, and on the completed restoration of the war-damaged Great Hall in 1963. But during these twilight years, he was increasingly withdrawn from life in general, and as a result, from the affairs of the University.[4]

Yet there was one final Bristolian episode involving Churchill, which may have owed more to its constituency politics than to its University; but

---

[2] A. Montague Browne, *Long Sunset: Memoirs of Winston Churchill's Last Private Secretary* (1995), p. 265; UoBSC DM 1571/21: PRM to WSC, 19, 26 March 1956; WSC to PRM, 22 March 1956.

[3] UoBSC DM 309: WSC to Sir Michael Adeane, 19 July 1958; A. Montague Browne to PRM, 21 July 1958, 25 October 1958; PRM to A. Montague Browne, 27 October 1958; A Montague Browne to PRM, 10 November 1958; WSC to PRM, 14 November 1958; WSC to Lord Sinclair, 19 November 1958.

[4] UoBSC DM 1571/27: A. Montague Browne to PRM, 14 February 1959; PRM to A. Montague Browne, 25 February 1959; DM 309: WSC to PRM, 1 May 1958, 2 June 1959; DM 2284/1/2: WSC to PRM, 6 February 1962; WSC to Lord Sinclair, 6 February 1962; DM 1571/21: Pro-Vice-Chancellor to A. Montague Browne, 9, 17 May 1962; A. Montague Browne to Pro-Vice-Chancellor, 15 May 1962; Restoration of the University Great Hall, Message from the Chancellor [December 1963]; PRM to WSC, 2 December 1963; *Evening Post*, 7 December 1963.

which was an important matter both locally and nationally, and could only have happened because the University had given him his unique and close connection with the City. In 1941, the Labour MP William Wedgwood Benn had been persuaded by Churchill and Clement Attlee to accept a peerage as Lord Stansgate, so as to strengthen his party's representation in the upper house. Nine years later, his only surviving son and heir, Anthony Wedgwood Benn (as he was then known), was elected Labour MP for the Bristol constituency recently vacated by Sir Stafford Cripps. Aware that on the death of his father, he would have no choice but to inherit his peerage, Wedgwood Benn determined to avoid that fate; and in his efforts to do so, he successfully enlisted Churchill's support.[5] In 1953, and clearly in response to a request from Wedgwood Benn, Churchill sent him a confidential letter stating that he was 'strongly in favour of sons having the right to renounce irrevocably the peerages they inherit from their fathers'. Soon after, Wedgwood Benn introduced a private member's bill, which would have allowed him to disclaim his peerage; and, having recently resigned from the prime ministership, Churchill authorised Benn to make use of the letter he had written two years before.[6] The bill was thrown out by the Lords, but in 1960, Lord Stansgate died, whereupon Wedgwood Benn was deemed automatically to have inherited his father's title and thus to be a member of the House of Lords and disbarred from the House of Commons. He was determined to fight, and a bill was eventually passed in 1963 that enabled those inheriting peerages to disclaim their titles. Wedgwood Benn promptly did so, and was re-elected to the Commons. But his legal expenses had been substantial, and via Montague Browne, Churchill contributed ten pounds to the 'Bristol fund' that was set up to support him.[7] It is a touching and perhaps unexpected late Churchill, late Bristol story.

Meanwhile, there were two remaining matters being dealt with by the University authorities in order to round off Churchill's Chancellorship. The first concerned the commissioning of an official portrait, which had initially been broached in the midst of the Second World War.

[5] R. Winstone (ed.), *Tony Benn, Years of Hope: Diaries, Letters and Papers, 1940–1962* (1994), pp. 175, 321, 376–7, 383–4, 413; T. Benn, *Out of the Wilderness: Diaries, 1963–67* (1987), pp. 208–9; T. Benn *et al.*, 'Churchill Remembered', in *Winston Churchill in the Twenty-First Century*, ed. D. Cannadine and R. Quinault (Cambridge, 2004), pp. 221–23.
[6] CHUR 2/506: WSC to A. Wedgwood Benn, 9 April 1955; A. Wedgwood Benn to WSC, 14 April 1955; Lord Salisbury to WSC, 22 April 1955.
[7] CHUR 2/506: A. Wedgwood Benn to WSC, 19 November 1959; A. Montague Browne to Wedgwood Benn, 24 November 1959; Wedgwood Benn to WSC, 1 December 1959, 14 March 1961, 8 April 1961, 7 October 1961, 5 July 1962; M. Zander to WSC, 13 September 1961; A. Montague Browne to Wedgwood Benn, 9 July 1962.

'The University', Thomas Loveday had explained to him in May 1944, 'much desire to have upon its walls a portrait of you by an artist of accomplishment, and eminence, and hopes that at some convenient time (which we realise is not likely to be in the immediate future) you will consent to sit for your portrait'. Churchill was 'very ready, if an occasion offered, to submit myself for a sitting'. But, he added, 'I am afraid I can make no promise in wartime, and will hardly be worth painting unless the war stops soon'.[8] Before 1955, he was always far too busy to make time for sittings, but thereafter, although he had the leisure, he no longer had the energy or the inclination, and in any case he was often out of the country, staying with friends in the south coast of France, or visiting Marrakesh, or cruising on the yacht owned by Aristotle Onassis; and so the official portrait never in fact materialised. To be sure, the University had already acquired a likeness 'from an American artist who is believed to have painted it from a photographic portrait', yet as the Vice-Chancellor explained to members of Council, such a derivative and generic work hardly constituted 'a satisfactory record in perpetuity of Sir Winston's tenure of office as Chancellor of the University'. But then, and entirely by chance, the opportunity arose to obtain a much better portrait of Churchill, appropriately clad in his robes as Chancellor of the University, which had been painted by Sir Frank Salisbury in 1943. The picture was acquired just a few months before Churchill's death, and it was purchased, as the official record stated, 'from private donations by members of Council who desired it to serve as a record for all time of their profound admiration of Sir Winston Churchill as statesman, writer, a great man of his generation, and a distinguished Chancellor of the University'.[9]

By then, Sir Philip Morris had already given serious attention to preparing for the day when Churchill would die, for he was not only a great man, but as the 'senior Chancellor of a British university', he had also held the office for more than a third of a century, and for more than half of the time that the University had been in existence. In February 1960, the Vice-Chancellor had raised the matter with Professor David Douglas, the eminent medieval historian and Dean of the Faculty of Arts. 'In the natural course of things', Morris noted, 'our Chancellor must come to the end of his life', and he asked Douglas to 'prepare in advance of the event a special number of the University *Gazette*', which could be made ready so as

---

[8] CHAR 2/520A-B: TTL to WSC, 14 May 1944; Minute by WSC, 29 May 1944; *C&G*, vii. 779, n. 1.
[9] UoBSC DM 1571/21: PRM to Miss E. Gilliatt, 2 September 1955; PRM to WSC, 19, 26 March 1956; WSC to PRM, 22 March 1956; DM 1571/27, PRM to Members of Council [undated, c 1964]; DM 15671/38, PRM to Oscar Nemon, 24 November 1964.

to be 'published... on or about the day of the funeral'.[10] Within little over a month, Douglas had completed his task, and on Churchill's death, the special edition of the *Gazette* duly appeared in January 1965: it paid tribute to his character and achievements, explained how he had been appointed in 1929, recounted how the University had developed in the years since then, described each of his visits as 'in truth royal occasions', provided vivid recollections of his conduct and behaviour at 'these gorgeous ceremonies', and listed the recipients of the honorary degrees he had personally bestowed.[11] In addition, the Vice-Chancellor sent a personal letter of sympathy and condolence to Lady Churchill, noting that 'our grief is tempered by pride and admiration, and also by gratefulness that we have been privileged to enjoy his wise and distinguished services over so long a period of time'; the Council recorded its 'deep sorrow in the death of Sir Winston Churchill, their sense of the honour and distinction he had brought to this University as its Chancellor... [and] their unbounded admiration for the inestimable service he rendered to his country and to the cause of freedom'; and on the day after his state funeral, there was a great memorial gathering in Bristol Cathedral, paying homage to the University's most illustrious Chancellor and to the City's most famous Honorary Freeman.[12]

Winston Churchill's death in January 1965 broke a much more significant link to the immediate past than his effective retirement from public life, and from the Bristol Chancellorship, had done more than ten years before. For his magnificent state funeral was not just the appropriate obsequy for the great man himself, but was also a requiem for Britain as a great power.[13] And while in many ways Churchill was a quintessential late Victorian, the late 1960s witnessed the first serious assault on the still-surviving Victorian moral code, with the de-criminalisation of abortion and homosexuality, and the reform of the divorce laws. At the University, the retirement of Sir Philip Morris, little more than a year after Churchill's death, was an

---

[10] UoBSC 1571/27: PRM to Professor David Douglas, 2 February 1960; Professor David Douglas to PRM, 19 March 1960.

[11] UoBSC DM 776: UoB, *Gazette*, 'Winston Spencer Churchill, Chancellor of the University of Bristol, 1929–1965' [January 1965], pp. 1, 10, 16–22.

[12] UoBSC DM 1571/38: PRM, press statement, 16 January 1965; PRM to Lady Churchill, 25 January 1965; DM 1143, UoB, Minutes of Council, July 1964 – July 1965, Meeting of 19 February 1965, pp. 103–06; DM 776, The Cathedral Church of the Holy and Undivided Trinity, Bristol, In Memoriam, Winston Leonard Spencer Churchill...Honorary Freeman of the City of Bristol, Chancellor of the University of Bristol [31 January 1965].

[13] D. Cannadine, *In Churchill's Shadow: Confronting the Past in Modern Britain* (2003), pp. 36–37; B. Levin, *The Pendulum Years: Britain and the Sixties* (1972), pp. 399–411; J. Dimbleby, *Richard Dimbleby* (1977), pp. 370–75; J. Morris, *Farewell the Trumpets: An Imperial Retreat* (Harmondsworth, 1978), pp. 545–57.

THE CATHEDRAL CHURCH
of
THE HOLY AND UNDIVIDED TRINITY, BRISTOL

IN MEMORIAM

WINSTON LEONARD SPENCER CHURCHILL
K.G., O.M., P.C., C.H., LL.D., F.R.S.

1874-1965

Honorary Freeman of the City of Bristol
Chancellor of the University of Bristol

SUNDAY, JANUARY 31st, 1965
at 11 o'clock a.m.

Figure 17. Order of Service, Bristol Cathedral, January 1965.

equally pronounced break with the past; and for the only occasion in its history, Bristol turned to a local grandee to be its next Chancellor, in the person of the duke of Beaufort. But he held the office for a mere five years, and was succeeded by Dorothy Hodgkin in 1970; while the turnover in Vice-Chancellors was even more rapid, with three of them holding office during the same period. Underlying and intensifying this uncertainty and instability at the very top of the University were serious student protests, which began earlier, and were more vehement and vigorous at Bristol, than at many other places. There were sit-ins and demonstrations, there was criticism that the University's decision-making processes were too secretive and too aloof; and some students even argued that the office of Chancellor was an indefensible anachronism that ought to be abolished. The protests would in the end die down, changes would be made to meet the criticisms that had been levelled, and during the Vice-Chancellorship of Sir Alec Merrison, which lasted from 1969 to 1984, there would be reform and recovery, stabilisation and consolidation, and (until the early Thatcher years) a further phase of growth and expansion.[14] But although the Wills Memorial Building still stood, restored, resplendent and magnificent at the top of Park Street, the fact remained that after the disruptions of the late 1960s, Bristol was no longer the University, in terms of its size and scale, or its structure and culture, that Loveday or Morris – or Churchill – would have recognised.

---

[14] *Bristol*, pp. 67–84.

Conclusion

Half a century since Churchill's death, there cannot be many people who are able to recall attending the memorial service held for him at Bristol Cathedral in January 1965; there are perforce even fewer who might remember his post-war appearances at the University; there must be scarcely anyone now living who was among the crowds which gathered to cheer him on his wartime visits in 1941 and 1945; and with the possible exception of his then-young train-bearers, it is almost inconceivable that there are any survivors from the degree congregations over which he presided during the 1930s, or from his installation as Chancellor. As for the notables on whom he bestowed honorary degrees – the local worthies, the eminent academics, the distinguished military figures, the senior Whitehall mandarins, the Labour and Conservative government ministers, the American Ambassadors, and the men from the British dominions and the British colonies – all those, too, have long since passed on. Moreover, none of the worlds from which these honorary graduates were drawn – local government, the universities, the armed forces, the civil service, the Commons or the Cabinet – stand as high in public esteem as they did in Churchill's day, while the 'special relationship' with the United States is not what it was, the British Empire has completely vanished, and the Commonwealth is but a pale shadow of its predecessor. All of which is but another way of saying that much of Churchill's world, in which he lived and moved and had his being, has long since disappeared; and in one real, regrettable but unavoidable sense, Churchill himself is disappearing, too. For fifty years on, in 2015, his long and extraordinary life is rapidly and inexorably passing from memory to history, and thus from recollection to reappraisal, and that is as true of him as Chancellor of the University of Bristol as it is of anything else – indeed, of everything else – that he did or that he said.

But as Churchill himself well knew, what is lost in personal knowledge and connection is gained in the lengthening perspective afforded by the passing of time, and from the vantage point of what is now the hundred-year-and-more history of the University, it is clear that Churchill's Bristol Chancellorship was, and remains, utterly unique. Beyond any doubt, all the men and women who have held that office, both before him and after him, have been persons of remarkable achievement and significant distinction in many different walks of life, and Bristol is, to its credit, unusual among English universities in having chosen two non-royal women as Chancellors, Dorothy Hodgkin and Baroness Hale, the present incumbent. But

Churchill stands out and above them all: in part because of the sheer length of his Chancellorship, unrivalled by any other holder of the office before or since; in part for being widely regarded as the 'greatest human being ever to occupy 10 Downing Street', and as the 'greatest Briton' ever to have lived; and in part because, and especially between 1941 and 1954, he performed the Chancellorship with a theatrical flair and consummate panache that were incomparable and inimitable.[1] To be sure, Churchill was not in his time the only British prime minister who was also chancellor of a British university. Two of his cabinet colleagues who subsequently followed him to 10 Downing Street held similar positions: Anthony Eden, later Lord Avon, was Chancellor of Birmingham University from 1945 to 1973, and Harold Macmillan, later Earl of Stockton, was Chancellor of Oxford University from 1960 to 1986. They may have played a more involved part in the detailed business of their respective universities, but neither of them held their offices for as long as Churchill did at Bristol, they were never global celebrities in the way that he eventually became, Eden's reputation went into irretrievable decline following his resignation after the Suez debacle of 1956, and Macmillan only blossomed as Oxford's Chancellor after he had ceased to be prime minister in 1963.[2]

All of which is but another way of saying that there has never been another Chancellor quite like Churchill, either at the University of Bristol, or, indeed, anywhere else. Very properly, the impact that any chancellor makes on the university over which he – or she – presides is formally limited to the ceremonial (and, increasingly, to the fund-raising) tasks they are expected to undertake and fulfil as 'great ornamentals'; and however much real influence they may also wield behind the scenes, the substance and reality of power lie mostly elsewhere, and that is as it should be.
[3]But in British universities, as in the British constitution, the 'dignified' parts, as distinct from the 'efficient' parts, undoubtedly possess a force and a significance all their own, and no one better caught or summarised Churchill's unique blend of dignified presence and forceful significance in the life of the University of Bristol than Sir Philip Morris, in these perceptive, appreciative and eloquent words, written in 1953:

> Even if the Chancellor of a University is a prime minister, and an exceptionally great prime minister at that, it is as a person that he inevitably becomes known

[1] R. Jenkins, *Churchill* (2001), p. 912.
[2] R. Rhodes James, *Anthony Eden* (1986), pp. 331, 609; A. Horne, *Harold Macmillan*, ii, *1957–1986* (New York, 1989), pp. 268–72, 597–602; R. Jenkins, *A Life at the Centre* (1991), pp. 605–7.
[3] D. Cannadine, *The Decline and Fall of the British Aristocracy* (1990), pp. 588, 601.

Conclusion

in his own University. In this case, the abiding impressions which, particularly of recent years, Sir Winston always left behind him, were of a man of rare and deep humanity who had a sure hold upon the importance and significance of human relationships. However preoccupied he might be by affairs of state, which inevitably followed him on his visits to Bristol, his mind and attention while he was in the university seemed to be concentrated upon the people he was meeting and upon the business in which he was taking part. In any final assessment of his place in history, his relationship to the University of Bristol deserves, as no doubt it will have, its own peculiar place.[4]

Five decades since his passing, there is still no 'final assessment' of Winston Churchill's 'place in history', and since he was a figure so unique, so extraordinary, so many-sided, so long-lived, and so admired but also so controversial, it seems highly unlikely that there ever will be – or that there ever could be or should be. But the fiftieth anniversary of the death of someone who was, among so many other things, Bristol's most famous and illustrious Chancellor, is surely the fitting occasion to recover, and the appropriate time to remember, the remarkable and revealing connection between that very great man and this very great university.

---

[4] W. Bagehot, *The English Constitution*, ed. M.Taylor (Oxford, 2001 edn.), pp. 9–10; UoBSC DM 1571/38: PRM, recollections of WSC, 22 July 1953, p. 6.

Index

Names are listed in the forms in which they appear in the text, eg 'Beaufort, 10th duke of', rather than 'Somerset, Henry (10th duke of Beaufort)'.

Alanbrooke, 1st viscount, 51
Alexander, Albert Victor, 33, 42, 52
Asquith, Herbert Henry, 9, 16
Attlee, Clement, 68

Balfour, Arthur, 9
Beaufort, 10th duke of, 41, 48, 72
Benn, Anthony Wedgwood, 68
Benn, William Wedgwood, 68
Bevin, Ernest, 33, 42–3, 52
Bondfield, Margaret, 17
Bridges, Sir Edward, 49
Bristol, University of
    receives Royal Charter, 13
    and other redbrick universities, 13
    post-war growth, 48
    Queen's Building, 58, 64
    student protests, 72
    Wills Hall of Residence, 17
    Wills Memorial Building, 17, 20, 33, 34–5, 58, 72
Broad, C. D., 51
Brook, Sir Norman, 61
Browne, Anthony Montague, 67, 68
Butler, Richard Austen, 9, 61, 62

Camrose, 1st viscount, 55
Cecil, Lord Hugh, 59
Chamberlain, Joseph, 13
Churchill, Lord Randolph, 5, 20, 21
Churchill, Sir Winston
    appointment as Chancellor, 1
    Chancellor of the Exchequer 1924–29, 6, 9, 20
    Chancellor's robes, 20
    Churchill Hall of Residence, 2
    death, 2, 70–1
    education, attitudes to, 8, 9, 18
    education and self-education, 5–9
    eightieth birthday, 60
    enters House of Commons, 8
    formally invited to Chancellorship, 16–17
    given freedom of the City of Bristol, 41
    installed as Bristol Chancellor, 17–18
    Iron Curtain speech, 45
    memorial in Queen's Building, 2
    memorial service, Bristol Cathedral, 2, 71, 73
    My Early Life, 5, 10, 12, 18, 21, 23, 48, 59
    in Bangalore, 7–8
    proposed as Chancellor, 15–17
    Rector of Aberdeen University 1914, 11
    visits to Bristol
        December 1929, 19–21
        June 1931, 25
        June 1935, 25
        July 1938, 28
        April 1941, 36–8
        April 1945, 41–3
        June 1946, 49
        July 1948, 50–1
        October 1949, 51–2
        December 1951, 55–9
        November 1954, 60–3
        Woodford controversy, 60–1
Churchill College, Cambridge, 1, 3
Clark, Sir Kenneth, 11

Colville, Jock, 36
Combined English Universities constituency, 60
Conant, James Bryant, 36
Cripps, Sir Stafford, 52–4, 57, 65, 68

de la Mare, Walter, 17
Douglas, David, 69
Douglas, Lewis Williams, 51–2
Dulverton, Lord, 58

Ede, James Chuter, 55
Eden, Anthony, 25, 27, 28, 74
Elizabeth II, Queen, 48, 61, 67
Essex, University of, 3

Fleming, Sir Alexander, 51
Franks, Sir Oliver, 40, 62
Fraser, Sir Ian, 57

George V, King, 15, 67
George VI, King, 48, 61
Great Depression, 19
Grigg, Sir James, 49

Haldane, Lord, 15, 16
Hale, Baroness, 73
Harriman, W. Averell, 39
Harrod, Sir Roy, 21
Hobhouse, Henry, 16, 18
Hodgkin, Dorothy, 72, 73
Horsbrugh, Florence, 9

Ismay, General Lord, 55

James, Robert Rhodes, 12

Kennedy, Joseph P., 29–30, 33
Keyes, Admiral Sir Roger, 17, 25

Lascelles, Sir Alan, 61
Laski, Harold, 11

Lee, John Clifford Hodges, 49
Lillicrap, Sir Charles, 55
Lindemann, Frederick, 11, 21
Lloyd, Lord, 25, 59
Loveday, Thomas, 14, 16, 18, 27–8 36–7, 40, 65, 69, 72

Macmillan, Harold, 74
McCormick, Sir William, 15–16
Mary, Queen, 15, 67
Menzies, Sir Robert, 36–8, 39–40
Merrison, Sir Alec, 72
Monckton, Sir Walter, 61
Moore, R.W., 51
Moran, Lord, 61, 62
Morris, Sir Philip, 1, 2, 40, 46, 50, 55, 57, 59, 65, 69, 70, 72

Onassis, Aristotle, 69

Percy, Lord Eustace, 9, 11
Portal, Viscount, 49
Runciman, Walter, 17, 24
Russell, A. E., 55

Sargent, John Singer, 6, 20
Shawcross, Sir Hartley, 61
Sibley, Thomas Franklin, 17
Snowden, Philip, 17
Somerville, Sir James, 49
Southwell, Sir Richard, 51
Strachey, Lytton, 12
Sutherland, Graham, 60

Tanner, Herbert, 48, 61, 62

Vaughan Williams, Ralph, 17, 55
Vian, Admiral Sir Philip Louis, 55

Wills, Henry Overton, 13–15
Winant, John Gilbert, 36–8, 39

www.ingramcontent.com/pod-product-compliance
Ingram Content Group UK Ltd.
Pitfield, Milton Keynes, MK11 3LW, UK
UKHW021834140426
5217IPUK00021B/1442